Introduction to the Sources and Founding of Alcoholics Anonymous

Dick B.'s Reference Titles on Alcoholics Anonymous History
Paradise Research Publications, Inc., Publisher;
Good Book Publishing Company, Distributor P.O. Box 837, Kihei, HI 96753-0837
Phone/Fax: (808) 874 4876, Email: dickb@dickb.com; URL: http://www.dickb.com/index.shtml

Publisher's January 1, 2007 List of Titles by Author Dick B.

A New Way In.
A New Way Out.
Anne Smith's Journal, 1933-1939.
By the Power of God: A Guide to Early A.A. Groups & Forming Similar Groups Today.
Cured!: Proven Help for Alcoholics and Addicts.
Dr. Bob and His Library.
God and Alcoholism: Our Growing Opportunity in the 21st Century.
Good Morning!: Quiet Time, Morning Watch, Meditation, and Early A.A.
Henrietta B. Seiberling: Ohio's Lady with a Cause.
Introduction to the Sources and Founding of Alcoholics Anonymous.
Making Known The Biblical History and Roots of Alcoholics Anonymous: A Fifteen-Year Research, Writing, Publishing and Fact Dissemination Project.
New Light on Alcoholism: God, Sam Shoemaker, and A.A.
The Akron Genesis of Alcoholics Anonymous.
The Books Early AAs Read for Spiritual Growth.
The Conversion of Bill W.
The First Nationwide A.A. History Conference - Comments of Dick B.
The Golden Text of A.A.: God, the Pioneers, and Real Spirituality.
The Good Book and The Big Book: A.A.'s Roots in the Bible.
The Good Book-Big Book Guidebook.
The James Club: The Original A.A. Program's Absolute Essentials.
The Oxford Group & Alcoholics Anonymous.
That Amazing Grace (Clarence & Grace S.).
Turning Point: A History of Early A.A.'s Spiritual Roots and Successes.
Twelve Steps for You: Let Our Creator, A.A. History, and the Big Book Be Your Guide.
Utilizing Early A.A.'s Spiritual Roots for Recovery Today.
When Early AA s Were Cured and Why.

Why Early A.A. Succeeded: The Good Book in Alcoholics Anonymous Yesterday and Today (a Bible Study Primer).

Available through other distributors

Hope: The Story of Geraldine O. Delaney, 2d ed. (Alina Lodge)
Our Faith Community A.A. Legacy (Dick B., Editor and compiler). (Came to Believe Publications)
Courage to Change (with Bill Pittman). (Hazelden)
Women Pioneers of AA (Dick B., contributor). (Hazelden)

Introduction
to
the Sources and Founding of
Alcoholics Anonymous

Dick B.

Paradise Research Publications, Inc.
Kihei, Maui, Hawaii

Paradise Research Publications, Inc.
PO Box 837
Kihei, HI 96753-0837
(808) 874-4876
Email: dickb@dickb.com
URL: http://www.dickb.com/index.shtml

Cover Design by American Creations of Maui

This Paradise Research Publications Edition is published by arrangement with Good Book Publishing Company, PO Box 837, Kihei, HI: 96753-0837

Note: All Bible verses quoted in this book, unless otherwise noted, are from the Authorized (or "King James") Version. The letters "KJV" are used when necessary to distinguish it from other versions.

ISBN: 1-885803-86-9

Contents

Introduction to the Sources and Founding of Alcoholics Anonymous

Divine Healing Has Been Man's Readily Available Helpmate for Centuries

Several Bible verses sufficiently illustrate the point:

> Bless the LORD, O my soul, and forget not all his benefits: Who forgiveth all thine iniquities; who healeth all thy diseases (Psalm 103:2-3)

> Then Peter opened his mouth, and said. . . How God anointed Jesus of Nazareth with the Holy Ghost and with power; who went about doing good, and healing all that were oppressed of the devil; for God was with him (Acts 10:34, 38)

> And Stephen, full of faith and power, did great wonders and miracles among the people (Acts 6:8)

> Then Philip went down to the city of Samaria and preached Christ unto them. And the people with one accord gave heed unto those things which Philip spake, hearing and seeing the miracles which he did. For unclean spirits, crying with loud voice, came out of many that were possessed with them: and many taken with palsies and that were lame, were healed (Acts 8:5-7)

> And he [Jesus] said unto them, Go into all the world, and preach the gospel to every creature. He that believeth and is baptized shall be saved; but he that believeth not shall be damned. And these signs shall follow them that believe; In my name shall they cast out devils; they shall speak with new tongues. They shall take up serpents; and if they drink any deadly thing, it shall not hurt them; they shall lay hands on the sick, and they shall recover. . . . And they went forth, and preached every where, the Lord working with them, and confirming the word with signs following. Amen. (Mark 16.15-18, 20)

See also Herbert Lockyer, D.D. *All The Miracles of the Bible: The Supernatural in Scripture – Its Scope and Significance.* (Grand Rapids, MI: Zondervan Publishing House, 1961); James Moore Hickson. *Heal The Sick* (London: Methuen & Co., Ltd., 1924) – one of the many healing books in Dr. Bob's Library; Pearcy Dearmer. M.A. *Body and Soul* (London: Sir Isaac Pitman & Sons, Ltd., 1909); J. R. Pridie, M.A. *The Church's Ministry of Healing* (London: Society For Promoting Christian Knowledge, 1926); Dick B. *When Early AAs Were Cured and Why, 3rd ed.* (Kihei, HI: Paradise Research Publications, Inc., 2006); *The First Nationwide Alcoholics Anonymous History Conference, 2d ed.* (Kihei, HI: Paradise Research Publications, Inc., 2006).

William D. Silkworth, M.D., was medical mentor of, and principal instructor for, Bill Wilson's ideas about alcoholism. But there is much more to the Silkworth/Wilson story, and the facts have only recently been brought to light largely by Dr. Silkworth's biographer, who wrote:

> Silkworth has not been given the appropriate credit for his position on spiritual conversion, particularly as it may relate to true Christian benefits. Several sources, including Norman Vincent Peale in his book *The Positive Power of Jesus Christ*, agree that it was Dr. Silkworth who used the term "The Great Physician" to explain the need in recovery for a relationship with Jesus Christ. If true, this reference to Jesus has all but been eliminated from Alcoholics Anonymous history. In the formation of AA, Wilson initially insisted on references to God and Jesus, as well as the Great Physician. As the fellowship grew, however, other members persuaded Bill that a purely Christian format would alienate many, keeping potential members away from joining the group. Silkworth challenged the alcoholic with an ultimatum. Once hopeless, the alcoholic would grasp hold of any chance of sobriety. Silkworth, a medical doctor, challenged the alcoholic with a spiritual conversion and a relationship with God as part of a program of recovery. His approach with Bill Wilson was no different. Dale Mitchel. *Silkworth: The Little Doctor Who Loved Drunks*. (MN: Hazelden, 2002), p. 50.

In an extensive article published in a medical journal on July 27, 1939, a few months after A.A.'s basic text was published, Silkworth himself said:

> That the chronic alcoholic has sometimes recovered by religious means is a fact centuries old. . . . [and speaking of A.A.'s program] he [the alcoholic must] recommit himself daily, or hourly if need be, to God's care and direction, asking for strength. . . . It is paramount to note that the religious factor is all important even from the beginning. Newcomers have been unable to stay sober when they have tried the program minus the Deity. Mitchel, *Silkworth*, pp, 159, 160, 162.

The Reverend Dr. Leslie D. Weatherhead published his monumental treatise on *Psychology, Religion, and Healing* (Nashville: Abingdon-Cokesbury Press, 1951) with a detailed study of Christ's healing miracles, healing in the Early Church, demon possession, and the falling away of the religious healing mission as the centuries moved on (pp. 29-101). But Weatherhead demonstrates with clarity and substantial evidence that divine healing was a fact much in existence from the much earlier centuries, just as Dr. Silkworth had stated. Weatherhead carries his study much further in listing all the various methods of healing that followed the apostolic age and continued to his own time.

Last but not least in importance are the writings in the early 1930's of the Rev. L.W. Grensted, M.A., D.D., Canon Theologian of Liverpool and Oriel Professor of the Philosophy of the Christian Religion in the University of Oxford. Of particular value is Grensted's *Psychology and God: A Study of The Implications of Recent Psychology For Religious Belief and Practice* (London: Longmans, Green and Co, 1931). In the period just before the founding of A.A. in 1935, Canon Grensted had already covered much of the ground it has taken me years to revive and rejuvenate. He discusses the theories of Saint Augustine, Dr. Carl Jung, Professor William James, and distinguished students of alcoholism, healing, the mind, and religion--Coue, Freud, Hickson, Leuba, Starbuck, Streeter, and others. Not only did Grensted become an admired figure by Oxford Group people, but also a strong advocate of the efficacy of divine healing. Even to the point that he wrote this of Mary Baker Eddy and her Christian Science:

> We may add that there will be no true psychotherapeutics unless the religious values preserved in Christian Science are retained. For the strength of Christian Science is that with all its simple minded

> credulity, its mass-suggestion, and its shirking of criticism, it has placed the love of God in the forefront of its teaching. It has helped men to forget their silly and unnecessary fears, their exaggerated anxieties in the contemplation of that love. And therein it has been true to the mind of Christ, and at least some of its work fully deserves to stand side by side with His. Grensted, *Psychology and God*, p. 108.

A.A.'s own conference approved literature records the fact that Bill Wilson and Dr. Bob both studied Christian Science for a time in hope of being cured by that religious means. To Wilson, it seemed "too metaphysical." For Dr. Bob, it was just one of the many works he studied on healing by religious means.

Religious Healing of Alcoholics in the Early 1930's and Before

A.A. admirers sometimes place so much emphasis on the dire plight of the alcoholic before A.A. that one might think nobody was getting sober or cured before A.A.'s time, whether by religious means or medical means. But A.A. pioneers made no such claim; nor would history have supported it. There were religious programs successfully at work at the very time Bill and Bob were oozing out of their drunkenness.

The Salvation Army: Since the late 1880's, the Salvation Army had been bringing salvation, shelter, sobriety, and individual ministry to suffering alcoholics and outcasts. Theirs was a very simple program of abstinence, acceptance of Christ, reliance on the Creator, Bible study, prayer, elimination of sin, and ministry by the healed for those still wallowing in the mire. See Harold Begbie, *Twice-Born Men: A Clinic in Regeneration* (New York: Fleming H. Revell Company, 1909); *The Gospel Truth: Life of William Booth, Founder and First General of the Salvation Army*, 2 vol. (New York: Macmillan, 1920). At the Yale Summer School of Alcohol Studies lectures of 1945, where Bill Wilson himself spoke, the Reverend Mc Peek, Executive Director of the Federation of Churches in Washington, D.C., described the Salvation Army's program in depth, and then added as to healing:

> Certain things may be held conclusive. Towering above them all is this indisputable fact: It is faith in the living God which has

> accounted for more recoveries from the disease than all other therapeutic agencies put together. Dick B., *When Early AAs Were Cured and Why,* pp. 1-3.

Not many years later, the Rev. Dr. Howard Clinebell, Professor Emeritus at Claremont School of Theology, a researcher of A.A. History, and an expert on pastoral counseling, expressed his belief:

> that the Army represents evangelistic therapy at its best and that some facilities have remarkable success in getting and keeping countless former homeless, low-bottom addicts sober and living constructive lives. Dick B. *A New Way In* (HI: Paradise Research Publications, 2006), pp. 45-46.

The Rescue Missions: In the years before A.A., the rescue and Gospel Missions were highly successful in developing their faith, surrender, conversion, and healing ideas in altar call services such as those in which Bill Wilson and his sponsor Ebby Thacher at the Calvary Rescue Mission participated in New York. Yet, over the objections of A.A. pioneer John Henry Fitzhugh Mayo, a tiny four-person New York contingent removed from A.A.'s basic text what they characterized as "dogma and doctrines" from the mission programs. Dick B. *The Conversion of Bill W.* (Kihei, HI: Paradise Research Publications, Inc., 2006), pp. 103-107; *A New Way In,* pp. 59-61; *A New Way Out* (Kihei, HI: Paradise Research Publications, Inc., 2006), pp. 40-41. This despite the well-known fact of that time, which was that both Ebby and Bill had very early pursued with success at the mission Dr. Carl Jung's thesis that religious cure for the medically incurable real alcoholic could still be achieved from a conversion. See, as to Jung's role, Cora Finch, *Carl Jung, a New England Family, and the Risk of Anecdote*, 2006 (http://www.stellarfire.org). Both Bill and Ebby participated in the evangelistic activities at Calvary Mission where Bible teaching, prayer, hymns, and altar calls led a willing penitent to the acceptance of Jesus Christ as Lord and Saviour. These religious activities followed or preceded testimonials during which a penitent like Bill and Ebby inevitably heard "Jesus saves," and was rescued from booze by turning to Christ. In fact, both Bill and Ebby were converted at that Calvary Rescue Mission run by Sam Shoemaker's church, and they said so. Dick B. *Real Twelve Step Fellowship History* (HI: Paradise Research Publications, Inc., 2006), p. 86. The Mission people often quipped that their facilities provided "soup, soap, and salvation" as well as sobriety to the thousands that passed through the dining halls, shelters, and conversion services.

The Evangelists and healers: There are many recorded instances of the pre-A.A. religious healing of drunks by evangelists such as Dwight L. Moody, Billy Sunday, John Hickson, Ethel Willitts, and certainly by Mary Baker Eddy's Christian Science. These preachers ministered directly to the unsaved, preached Jesus Christ, and—except for Eddy and her divine science—claimed healings at the hands of the "Great Physician." Their writings appear among the books AAs studied for help. See Dick B., *Dr. Bob and His Library*, 3rd and *The Books Early AAs Read for Spiritual Growth*, 7th ed. For the many, widespread references to Jesus Christ as the "Great Physician" throughout the years, see Dick B. *The Conversion of Bill W.*, pp. 62-70.

The many healing movements: In the 1930's, and for many years before that, there were still a host of groups calling on God for healing. Even of alcoholics! They could be found at tent revivals, temperance meetings, temperance groups, anti-saloon efforts, Holiness and Pentecostal convocations, Awakenings, and gatherings of others pledging abstinence. All achieved some mark in the realm of abstinence. Most involved God and a religious element. Most, for a variety of reasons, have been criticized as ineffective or at least been subjected to question as to effectiveness. Skeptics had such notions as "the age of miracles is gone;" any healings were merely of a psychological nature—not physical; and there were charlatans at work. But the healings occurred; and hundreds of thousands were attracted to the meetings. See *John G. Lake: The Complete Collection of His Life Teachings.* Compiled by Roberts Liardon. (Tulsa, OK: Albury Publishing, 1999); Kenneth O. Brown. *Holy Ground Too: The Camp Meeting Family Tree* (Hazleton, PA: Holiness Archives, 1997); Roger A. Bruns. *Preacher: Billy Sunday and Big-Time American Evangelism* (Chicago: University of Illinois Press, 1992); C. Douglas Weaver. *The Healer-Prophet: William Marrion Branham, A Study of the Prophetic in American Pentecostalism* (Macon, GA: Mercer University Press, 2000); *T. L. Osborn. Believers in Action* (Tulsa, OK: Osborn Publishers, 2000); Julius Stadsklev. *William Branham: A Prophet Visits South Africa* (MN: 1952). F. F. Bosworth. *Christ The Healer* (Grand Rapids, MI: Fleming H. Revell, 1973). For the centuries of all such healings, see Dick B. *The First Nationwide Alcoholics*

Anonymous History Conference, 2d ed. (Kihei, HI: Paradise Research Publications, Inc., 2006), pp. 5-19.

The conversion and healing of Bill W.'s Grandpa Willie: Odd it is that AAs have sometimes expressed contempt of religion, churches, and revivals and yet have never heard that Bill Wilson's grandfather Willie Wilson, through his conversion on Mount Aeolus in Vermont, was healed of alcoholism and never drank again to the date of his death. See Dick B. *The Conversion of Bill W.;* Susan Cheever. *My Name is Bill. Bill Wilson: His Life and the Creation of Alcoholics Anonymous* (NY: Washington Square Press, 2004), p. 17. See also Richard M. Riss. *A Survey of 20th Century Revival Movements in North America* (Peabody, Mass: Hendrickson Publishers, 1988); Roberts Liardon. *God's Generals: Why They Succeeded and Why Some Failed* (Tulsa, OK: Albury Publishing, 1996). In fact, it was probably the upshot of the work of the evangelists, the revivals, and the healers—plus Grandpa Willie Wilson's conversion and victory over drunkenness that, years later, made Grandson Bill a ready experimenter with conversion—his own.

Thus ends my brief discussion of those who looked to God and asked for help in the name of Jesus for many many years before A.A. was founded. And then there was an A.A. Society founded on a new approach. A.A. certainly pointed to medicine as its source of information that real alcoholics were "medically incurable." Both Bill Wilson and Dr. Bob had tried that medicinal route. A.A. also chose—perhaps because of its initial adventures with the non-sectarian Oxford Group, their teams, and their individual life-changing approaches—to work outside structured religious boundaries—though still recommending religious comradeship and church attendance in its successful Akron program. In a very real sense, and just as Bill Wilson declared, AAs borrowed from a variety of sources and practices—all centered around the love, service, protective zeal, and comradery generated by those with like problems and healed by the proposed solutions. There probably had been a mid-life disdain by Bill and by Bob for reliance on what some might have characterized as a judgmental church structure and ineffective medical techniques. Nonetheless it was Dr. Bob's long-time relationship with his Creator and with the Bible and Bill Wilson's early conversion experience that led both founders to see that reliance on the Creator was the force that could bring them out of the mire and into a new life. See 2 Corinthians 5:17—an oft-quoted verse about the new man in Christ. It was about their Heavenly Father, about changing their thinking, language, and actions through love, and about their individually serving God and others, said Dr. Bob. And those were the basic tools used to build their new kind of society. Dick B. *When Early AAs Were Cured and Why.*

There Was No Mutual or Agreed Common A.A. Source Nor any Specific Plan For Recovery. But there were Five Fairly Distinct Historical Parts of A.A.'s Founding Process and Program

I firmly believe that an informed knowledge of, and practical utilization of, the real history of early Alcoholics Anonymous for recovery today definitely requires a knowledge of the five distinctly different elements (discussed below) that make up the whole picture.

Part One: The Akron Genesis Period—Commencing in Dr. Bob's Childhood and Continuing until the Pioneers' Prayers at the home of T. Henry Williams

***Christian Endeavor Roots*:** The major principles and practices of the Akron program appear to be a product of Dr. Bob's youth. The United Christian Endeavor Movement began in a Congregational Church in Williston, Maine about the time of Bob's birth. It was formed to bring young people back to support their individual churches. It embodied Confession of Christ, Conversion Meetings, Bible Study Meetings, Prayer Meetings, Quiet Hour, symbolized by Love and Service. And from these roots, Dr. Bob acquired his immense knowledge of the Bible and Christian principles in action. Over the many years following 1880, Christian Endeavor featured the dynamics of evangelists like Dwight L. Moody, Billy Sunday, and the writer Charles Sheldon. Its worldwide membership grew to 3,500,000. Its members included eight U.S. presidents. See Dick B. *The James Club and The Original A.A. Program's Absolute Essentials* (Kihei, HI: Paradise Research Publications, 2006); *When Early AAs Were Cured and Why.*

***The first significant series of events, centered around Akron, began with the unusual Russell Firestone conversion and deliverance from liquor in 1931*:** A unique catalyst for the Akron birth was the conversion to Christ of Russell Firestone, a real alcoholic and an heir of the Akron Firestone Rubber clan. Russell's decision for Christ occurred in a train compartment during Russell's return from Denver to Akron under the tutelage of Rev. Samuel M. Shoemaker. Russell was miraculously healed. Then followed about two years of Russell's witnessing in company with his Oxford Group friend James Newton. In 1933, the grateful Firestone family held huge social and religious events with testimonies in church pulpits, news articles, and meetings throughout the City of Akron. There were widely printed and oral testimonies that people could be changed through Bible study, prayer, quiet time, relying on the Creator for strength and guidance, and then sharing their practices with those still needing "change." Dick B. *The*

Akron Genesis of Alcoholics Anonymous, 2d ed. (Kihei, HI: Paradise Research Publications, 1998).

The second series of Akron events involved Dr. Bob's attempts at sobriety, sparked by the Firestone events of 1933**:** As a direct result of the Firestone testimonies, Dr. Bob, his wife Anne, his friend Henrietta Seiberling, and Mr. and Mrs. T. Henry Williams soon began attending the West Hill Oxford Group meeting in Akron. For over two and a half years, these people met as a small fellowship consisting of Oxford Group people, alcoholics, and their families. Later, some called it "The alcoholic squad." *DR BOB and the Good Oldtimers* (NY: Alcoholics Anonymous World Services, Inc, 1980), p. 100. And, persuaded in substantial part by his contact with these people, Dr. Bob resumed his childhood study and training in the Bible; frequented church; prayed; and read an immense amount of Christian and Oxford Group literature. But Bob stayed drunk—for the simple reason that he didn't want to quit. Dick B. *Henrietta B. Seiberling: Ohio's Lady with a Cause,* 4th ed. (Kihei, HI: Paradise Research Publications, 2006).

Bob's surrender at the T. Henry Williams home. Feverishly working for Bob's sobriety, Henrietta Seiberling finally convened a no-nonsense meeting of the little group, passed on to Dr. Bob God's revelation to her that Dr. Bob must not touch one drop of liquor. At the meeting, Henrietta Seiberling extracted from Bob the admission that he was a "secret drinker;" and then Henrietta led the tiny fellowship and Bob himself to prayer on their knees on the carpet of the meeting at T. Henry's where all besought God's help for Dr. Bob's problem. See T. Willard Hunter. *"It Started Right There" Behind the Twelve Steps and the Self-help Movement*. (Oregon: Grosvenor Books, 1994); Dick B. *Henrietta B. Seiberling*.

But God's solution was far more than any of the participants could have expected that evening of the prayers and of Dr. Bob's surrender. A new wind was blowing from New York.

Part Two: The New York Conversion Period Commencing Primarily at Calvary Rescue Mission and Continuing Until Bill's Desperate Telephone Call to Henrietta Seiberling in Akron

The New York conversions—which had really bombed as far as Bill Wilson's witnessing was concerned—seemingly have no connection with the Akron prayers for Dr. Bob. But who can say? And let's review the chain of events that occurred before and at the time Bill Wilson arrived in Akron in 1935 on an ill-fated business venture. Some in today's A.A. might ask of this series of developments: "Was it odd, or was it God?"

The Carl Jung prescription of conversion as the solution for alcoholism: In despair after unsuccessful, extended treatment for alcoholism with the famed psychiatrist Dr. Carl Gustav Jung in Switzerland, Rowland Hazard of Rhode Island returned to Dr. Jung and sought special help for his seemingly hopeless drinking problem. Jung stated, however, that the only solution he knew for Rowland's "mind of a chronic alcoholic" was cure by religious means through a conversion. Dick B., *The Conversion of Bill W.* Jung named a couple of other approaches as well.

The Rowland Hazard factor: Rowland Hazard left Jung and sought an unusual type of help in the Oxford Group, learned their principles and practices, and achieved sobriety by following their life-changing program. I know of no proof that he had a conversion as such. But heeding the O.G. stress on the duty to witness to, and help others with, Christian outreach, Rowland rescued from incarceration a hopeless Albany drunk named Edwin T. Thacher (known as Ebby). Mel B., *Ebby: The Man Who Sponsored Bill W.* (MN: Hazelden). Rowland taught Ebby the Jung conversion thesis, the Oxford Group principles and practices, and lodged Ebby in the Calvary Rescue Mission run by Rev. Sam Shoemaker's Calvary Episcopal Church in New York. *Pass It On* (NY: Alcoholics Anonymous World Services, 1984).

***Ebby Thacher's conversion to Christ at the Rescue Mission altar, his apparent immediate recovery, followed by his witness to Bill Wilson*:** Few seemed to know it, but, *before Ebby's first visit with Bill in 1934*, Bill Wilson had been talking extensively with his psychiatrist Dr. William D. Silkworth during Bill's hospitalizations at Towns Hospital in New York. Silkworth had reassured Bill that he could be healed by the Great Physician Jesus Christ. Out of the blue, Bill's old friend and drinking buddy Ebby visited Bill and told Bill that he had "got religion," had been to the altar at Calvary Mission, had been reborn, and knew that God had done for him what he could not do for himself. Dick B., *Turning Point: A History of Early A.A.'s Spiritual Roots and Successes*. (Kihei, HI: Paradise Research Publications, 1997); *Real Twelve Step Fellowship History* (Kihei, HI: Paradise Research Publications, 2006).

***Apparently seeking help from the Great Physician, and desirous of the conversion and healing Ebby had experienced at the Rescue Mission, Bill Wilson sought out the mission altar and made a decision there for Christ*:** Bill soon proclaimed, as Ebby had, that he (Bill) also had "got religion," been "born again," and would then seek more help at Towns Hospital. At Towns, Bill decided to call on the Great Physician for healing. Bill then reviewed with Ebby some of the Oxford Group principles, cried out for God's help, had a miraculous conversion experience (as attested by Silkworth and Bill's wife), and then sought validation that the experience was real and not just an hallucination. Dick B., *The Conversion of Bill W.; Bill W. My First Forty Years: An Autobiography by the Co-Founder of Alcoholics Anonymous (MN: Hazelden,* 2000), pp. 139-149.

***William James's book "The Varieties of Religious Experience" was one with which Jung was apparently conversant, which Oxford Groupers had read, which Silkworth had read, and which contained dramatic eye witness accounts of how men had found God at missions through seeking Jesus Christ as their Saviour*:** Bill was given the William James book, either by Rowland Hazard or by Ebby. He devoured it over a period of several hours and "kept at it all day." There he read the many accounts of conversion experiences at missions and elsewhere. And he concluded that his conversion had been genuine. He'd experienced one of the very solutions Jung had prescribed. He'd had a conversion experience. He never drank again.

See extensive documentation in Dick B., *The Conversion of Bill W.*; Bill Wilson, *Bill W. My First Forty* Years, pp. 150-159; Mel B. *New Wine: The Spiritual Roots of the Twelve Step Miracle* (MN: Hazelden, 1991).

Persuaded by Ebby's witnessing, by the Oxford Group precepts, and by his own validation of the Jung/James conversion solution, Bill immediately became a messenger on fire with his story, but he wound up licking his wounds in Akron. In New York, Bill had preached his message at the Calvary Rescue Mission, at Towns Hospital, and at Oxford Group meetings. *Bill W. My First Forty Years*, p. 161. And for the little discussed or recognized content of his probable message, see his own words—"the Lord has been so wonderful to me, curing me of this terrible disease"—on page 191, *Alcoholics Anonymous*, 4th ed. (New York: Alcoholics Anonymous World Services, Inc.) and *DR. BOB*, p. 83. But not one person seemed persuaded by Bill's testimony, And not one achieved sobriety at Bill's own hands. *The Language of the Heart: Bill W.'s Grapevine Writings* (NY: The AA Grapevine, Inc., 1988), pp. 246-247; Mitchel, *Silkworth*, pp. 108-109 (stating, "Once Wilson had failed miserably to sober up the world, he turned to Silkworth for help" . . . . Bill Wilson himself wrote of: "...six months of failure on my part to dry up any drunks. . ." And Bill then set out for Akron on an ill-fated stock transaction and found himself beset with an urge to drink. Remembering the Oxford Group slogan, "You have to give it away to keep it," Bill laboriously sought out a drunk, just "any" drunk, to help. And he eventually phoned Henrietta Seiberling. Dick B., *Henrietta B. Seiberling: Ohio's Lady with a Cause* (Kihei: HI: Paradise Research Publications, Inc., 2004) pp. 39-42.

***Henrietta Seiberling certainly understood Dr. Bob's alcoholism. She understood the Oxford Group's "sharing for witness" principle. She understood Bill's stated need to pass on to another his own experience in overcoming drinking. Most important of all, she realized that the prayers of the Oxford Group people and others for Dr. Bob had been answered in an unusual and unexpected way*:** She proclaimed of Bill that he was "manna from heaven" and arranged for Bill and Bob to meet each other at her Gate Lodge home the next day. Bill's lone and unsuccessful endeavors in New York were about to end. A.A.'s founding began to take shape and followed after a number of days.. Dick B. *Henrietta B. Seiberling,* pp. 43-45.

Part Three: The Original A.A. Program That Akron Developed

For a general presentation of this material, see *DR. BOB and the Good Oldtimers*; Dick B. *The Akron Genesis of Alcoholics Anonymous; Real Twelve Step Fellowship History*; *The James Club and the Original A.A. Program's Absolute Essentials*, and *Henrietta B. Seiberling: Ohio's Lady with a Cause.*

The Specifics of What the Pioneers Did in Akron

First, they would locate a "real" alcoholic who needed help, wanted help, and would do whatever was expected of him**:** In the case of each of the first three AAs—Bill Wilson, Dr. Bob Smith, and Bill Dotson—someone had actually gone searching for each of those three men as "pigeons" needing help. Later, wives and relatives would sometimes bring a new man to Dr. Bob for help. Sometimes drunks appeared on the scene and asked for help. But searching out and "qualifying" the new person as one who was serious and willing was a critical part of the new program. The prospect was interrogated to verify that he was a real alcoholic and was willing to go to any length to get well. And that very outreach itself contributed mightily both to the newcomer's possible success and to the continued sobriety of his messenger/helper. All learned in those experiences that you can't make a drunk quit unless he wants to; but you can provide him with a personal testimony of success that has clout and compelling attraction. See *DR. BOB*, pp. 108-110.

They usually hospitalized the newcomer for about seven days**:** Hospitalization and/or medical help for a brief period was virtually a "must" for almost all the early A.A. members. *DR. BOB*, p. 102. Then, as now, there was danger of seizures, severe shaking, injury to self, serious illness, and disorientation. Medical monitoring was considered prudent. During that period, only a Bible was allowed in the hospital room. Medications were administered. There were daily visits and lengthy talks by Dr. Bob with each patient. There were regular visits by recovered pioneers who apprised the newcomer of their own stories and successes. Just prior to discharge, there was a visit to the newcomer by Dr. Bob. He may have covered additional points about alcoholism, such as they were known at that time. Primarily, however, he asked the new person to acknowledge his belief in the Creator. If there was an affirmative answer, Dr. Bob required the patient to make a "surrender" to Christ on his knees and join Dr. Bob in a prayer. And release from the hospital followed. See *DR. BOB*, p. 144; Dick B. *That Amazing Grace* [Clarence and Grace Snyder] (Kihei, HI: Paradise Research Publications, 1996).

The Akron fellowship often offered food, shelter, and support in the home of some pioneer family: The two homes that first come to mind are those of Dr. Bob and his wife Anne Smith, and Wally G. and his wife Annabelle. In a sense, these Akron live-in arrangements represented the first "half-way" houses as they are often called today. The Wilsons had previously tried it in New York, but with no success whatever. Recovery work in Akron did not begin or take place in groups or meetings or treatment centers; nor in rehabs or therapy or confinement. It took place primarily in Christian homes, and that, in itself, constituted a very different situation from the program of the Oxford Group where Bill Wilson had previously cut his teeth in the New York area. The Akron live-in newcomers were fed, sheltered, and helped with their healing opportunity. *DR. BOB;* Dick B., *The Akron Genesis.*

As detailed in my title, *The Akron Genesis of Alcoholics Anonymous*, Akron pioneer efforts took place primarily in the homes of people like Dr. Bob and Anne Smith. And in these homes, there were: (1) Daily religious get-togethers. (2) Bible studies and the reading of Christian literature and devotionals circulated by Dr. Bob and his wife. (3) Quiet Times held by each of the individuals who then prayed, studied the Bible, and sought God's guidance on their own. (4) Morning Quiet Time meetings led by Dr. Bob's wife for AAs and their families who listened to Anne teach from the Bible, prayed together, heard Anne share from her spiritual journal, discussed its contents with those present, and many then sought guidance from God for the day. One historian remarked: "Anne served God and Scripture to all who gathered at her daybreak meal." Mary C. Darrah. *Sister Ignatia* (Chicago: Loyola University Press, 1992), pp. 114-116. (5) Residents frequently discussed problems and Biblical solutions with Dr. Bob, Henrietta Seiberling, T. Henry Williams, and Anne Smith. And those who stayed over many days and nights, in this or that home, broke bread, lived, and fellowshipped together—much as the early Christians did as described in the Book of Acts. (6) Once a week the pioneers held a "regular" Wednesday meeting with "real" surrenders upstairs after the manner of James 5:15-16. (7) Pioneers also utilized a few of some twenty-eight Oxford Group life-changing practices such as Inventory, Confession, Conviction, and Restitution. Dick B. *The Oxford Group and Alcoholics Anonymous.* (8) They then arranged visits to newcomers at the hospital. (9) They recommended church attendance by most. (10) They enjoyed social, religious, and family fellowship. (11) And it all began again.

***There was one "Regular" weekly meeting on Wednesdays at the home of T. Henry and Clarace Williams in Akron*:** Though it originally began as an Oxford Group meeting, it was not conducted like most Oxford Group meetings. Its members—Oxford Group members, alcoholics, wives and children—were there to help alcoholics get well by spiritual means. And that was never a significant Oxford Group objective; and there was even a separateness between Groupers and alkies (*DR. BOB*, pp. 136, 142, 158). Host T. Henry Williams called the meeting a "clandestine lodge" of the Oxford Group because it differed so much from the movement Frank Buchman and Sam Shoemaker were leading in the East and abroad and in which a few East Coast AAs like Bill Wilson were participating. Also, before the Wednesday meeting, leaders such as Dr. Bob, Anne, Henrietta Seiberling, and Mr. and Mrs. Williams would hold a Monday "setup" meeting where God's guidance was sought as to who should lead the Wednesday meeting and what its topic should be. On Wednesdays, there were none of the conventional Oxford Group testimonials nor were there any of what have today become alcoholic drunkalogs. The regular meeting opened with a prayer. Scripture was read, then group prayer, and then a brief group guidance circle. The members discussed a selected topic—whether from the Bible, a devotional, or a subject involving living by Biblical principles. The discussion was led by someone such as Dr. Bob, Henrietta Seiberling, or T. Henry Williams. There was intense focus on the study and discussion of the Bible's Book of James, Sermon on the Mount, and 1 Corinthians 13. See Dick B. *The James Club*. There was a special time for "real" surrenders upstairs for the newcomers. See Dick B. *Henrietta B. Seiberling*, p. 51. Following those, arrangements were made downstairs for some in the group to visit newcomers at the Akron City Hospital. The meeting closed with the Lord's Prayer; socializing; and the exchange of Christian literature displayed on tables for the taking. There had been no drunkalogs. No Steps. No Big Book. No texts at all. Just the Bible and devotionals like *The Upper Room* and the specially valued lessons taught from James, Corinthians, and Matthew.

"Real Surrenders" to Christ, several Oxford Group practices, counseling with the Smiths and Henrietta Seiberling, study of Christian literature, and attending church:

(1) Real surrenders: In order to belong to the Akron fellowship, newcomers had to make a "real surrender." This was akin to the altar call at rescue missions or a confession of Christ with other believers in churches and revivals, except that it was a very small, private, ceremony which took place upstairs and away from the regular meeting. Four A.A. old-timers (Ed Andy, J. D. Holmes, Clarence Snyder, and Larry Bauer) have all independently verified orally and in writing that the Akron surrenders required acceptance of Jesus Christ as Lord and Saviour. Dick B. *Real Twelve Step Fellowship History.* Those conversions took place at the regular Wednesday meeting upstairs in the manner described in James 5:15-16. Kneeling, with "elders" at his side, the newcomer accepted Christ and, with the prayer partners, asked God to take alcohol out of his life and to help, guide, and strengthen him to live by cardinal Christian teachings such as those in the Oxford Group's rendition of the essence of what they felt to be the four absolute moral standards taught by Jesus—The Four Absolutes—Honesty, Purity, Unselfishness, and Love.

(2) Life-changing practices from the Oxford Group: Not so clear as to Akron is just how many of its pioneers completed such Oxford Group life-changing practices as Inventory, Confession, Conviction, and Restitution though there is mention of a *few* of the twenty-eight ideas [*DR. BOB,* p. 179]. Also of such guides as are found in the anonymously authored, *What Is The Oxford Group?,* which, though not the Oxford Group bible, as some think it to be, does discuss several of the O.G. principles and practices.

(3) Counseling, Bible Study, Life problems, Family issues: Men and women received counseling from Bob and Anne Smith, Henrietta Seiberling, and T. Henry Williams. Bill himself said, "Anne and Henrietta infused much needed spirituality into Bob and me." *The Language of the Heart: Bill W.'s Grapevine Writings*, p. 357. Pioneers frequently studied or listened to the reading of Scripture, prayed, and discussed practical matters like jobs and family difficulties. Anne Smith, for example, worked extensively with new people and their families. Darrah, *Sister Ignatia*, pp. 114-118.

(4) Widespread reading of Christian literature: Dr. Bob, His wife Anne, Henrietta Seiberling, and others fed AAs and their families a wide variety of literature on the Bible, prayer, healing, love, forgiveness, the guidance of God, the life of Christ, Shoemaker's writings, Oxford Group books, and daily study topics. These were circulated around the fellowship and read by alcoholics and family members alike. Dick B. *The Books Early AAs Read for Spiritual Growth*, 7th ed.; *Dr. Bob and His Library*, 3rd ed.

(5) The Church Option: Though A.A. literature is devoid of significant mention of church, the Frank Amos reports to Rockefeller disclose that attendance at a church of one's choice was recommended. There is particular evidence that Roman Catholics were in touch with their own priests. See Dick B., *That Amazing Grace;* Darrah, *Sister Ignatia.* And that the Akron leaders—Bob, Anne, Henrietta, and Mr. and Mrs. Williams—all attended churches in Akron.

Quiet Times: (held by individuals, by the group, and by the early birds in the morning with Anne Smith). The first Biblical condition for receiving revelation from God is *not* "listening" to God. The first condition of effective communication by a believer with the Creator is the establishing of one's standing as a child of God by accepting Jesus Christ as Lord and Saviour. See 1 Corinthians 1:17-31; 2:1-16 as to the wisdom of God. With that accomplished, the new Christian is a member of the body of Christ, able to communicate with God and His son, and endowed with the ability to understand spiritual matters the "natural man" cannot comprehend. See 1 Corinthians 2:9-16. Hence, this was a vital part of the Akron program–evidenced by the "surrender" at the hospital and certainly the "real surrender" in the homes. Then, for these born-again believers, Quiet Time consisted of reading the Bible, prayer to and seeking revelation from God, use of devotionals like *The Upper Room*, utilizing *Anne Smith's Journal* for teaching and instruction, and reading Christian literature such as Henry Drummond's *The Greatest Thing in the World,* Nora Smith Holm's *The Runner's Bible, The Upper Room,* and various studies of the Sermon on the Mount by Oswald Chambers, Glenn Clark, Harry Emerson Fosdick, Emmet Fox, and E. Stanley Jones. For more on Quiet Time principles and practices, see Dick B. *Good Morning: Quiet Time, Morning Watch, and Meditation in A.A.*, 2d ed. (Kihei, HI: Paradise Research Publications, Inc., 1998); *Making Known the Biblical History and Roots of Alcoholics Anonymous*, 3rd ed. (Kihei, HI; Paradise Research Publications, Inc., 2006), pp. 67-68; Howard Rose, *The Quiet Time* (NY: Oxford Group at 61 Gramercy Park,

North, 1937); Kenneth Belden. *Beyond the Satellites: Is God Speaking or Are We Listening* (London: Grosvenor Books, 1987).

Intensive personal work with newcomers: Dr. Bob was called the "Prince of Twelfth Steppers" and worked personally with over 5000 alcoholics. *Co-Founders of Alcoholics Anonymous: The Biographical Sketches; Their Last Talks* (NY: Alcoholics Anonymous World Services, Inc., 1972, 1975). Visits with newcomers by those who had already made the grade were a regular occurrence in Akron. Though Bill's own outreach efforts yielded little fruit in the East, compared to the results in Akron, Bill was the original, vigorous hustler—seeking out new people at Oxford Group meetings, Towns Hospital, and Calvary Rescue Mission. "He had been so impressed that a true agnostic like himself could find a relationship with God that. . . He would go to bars, hospitals—anywhere he might find a drunk to convert." Mitchel, *Silkworth*, p. 52. Topping even that was the unquestioned, liveliest 12th Stepping by young Clarence H. Snyder. Before he formed the Cleveland group, Clarence was bringing alcoholics down to Akron on a regular basis. In Cleveland, Clarence was a dynamo seeking out drunks under bridges and with newspaper ads, taking them through Step classes, and getting new groups going. Later, his outreach continued through spiritual retreats for AAs and their families where "coming to believe" was the featured object. See Dick B., *That Amazing Grace*. Cleveland groups grew from one to thirty in a year. Darrah, *Sister Ignatia*, pp. 156-157. The documented Cleveland success rate was 93%. *DR. BOB*, p. 261. Clarence sponsored hundreds and hundreds—finally becoming the AA with the longest period of sobriety. See Three Old-timer Clarence Snyder Sponsees, *Our Legacy to the Faith Community.*

Self-government, self-leadership, and self-support within membership groups: Both Dr. Bob and Bill were raised in the tradition of the New England Congregational denominations. This meant that each church was governed by its members. It was supported by its members. And it was accountable to no higher power, official, office, or administration than the rule and vote of its own congregation. Dick B. *The Conversion of Bill W., pp. 10-11.* Whatever the way by which this concept reached A.A., this system became the rule for local A.A. groups though Dr. Bob was undeniably the "leader" in Akron in the early pioneer days. At the same time, Bob was always opposed to transferring "control" of the A.A. fellowships to New York or some central administration there. Cheever. *My Name is Bill*, pp. 197-198.

Helping wives and families. Early AAs were male. But the early A.A. meetings in Akron were family affairs. Alkies, their wives, and their children would attend the meetings at the home of T. Henry and Clarence Williams. Oxford Group activists did the same thing. Henrietta Seiberling made sure all her children attended some of the meetings. The Smith kids attended many. Wives of members worked shoulder-to-shoulder with their husbands. Thus the work of T. Henry had the help of his wife Clarace. The work of Dr. Bob, that of Anne. The work of Wally G., that of his wife Annabelle. The work of Tom Lucas, that of his wife. And the work of Clarence Snyder, that of his wife Dorothy. But there were special needs of wives of alcoholics that began to be recognized right away. Anne Smith was at the head of the pack in meeting them. In early 1936, she organized a "Women's Group: for wives of alcoholics. Mary C. Darrah. *Sister Ignatia* (Chicago, Loyola University Press, 1992), pp. 118, 121-122. Throughout early A.A. personal stories and A.A. histories and biographies, you find remarks that Anne was legendary with newcomers and was especially kind to wives. She was particularly helpful to Lois Wilson time and time again. Her crown jewel, of course, was her material in *Anne Smith's Journal, 1933-1939*, 3rd ed. (Kihei, HI: Paradise Research Publications, Inc., 1938) which she wrote and used for teaching during all of A.A.'s formative years. Anne's journal is filled with materials as suitable for dealing with the problems of family as with the alcoholic himself. But it is quite clear that Anne Smith, Bob, Bill to some extent, and later, even Lois realized that the special problems of what some now call "the family disease" of alcoholism needed to be addressed, both for the sake of individuals, of those who suffer, and for A.A. itself. Even Lois Wilson huddled in New York with her little "kitchen group" for quite some time before the seeds of Al-Anon and its Family Groups began to appear and take root. See William G. Borchert. *The Lois Wilson Story: When Love Is Not Enough* (MN: Hazelden, 2006), pp. 188-191, 226, 235-237, 241, 244-245, 265-268.

Then when Bill and Bob were together: I have several times quoted or summarized the statements of Bob and Bill together on the platform of the Shrine Auditorium in Los Angeles in 1943. Their remarks were reported in the March, 1943 issue of *The Tidings*. About 4500 AAs and their families were present. Bill spoke about the importance of Divine Aid, the religious element in A.A., and prayer. Dr. Bob spoke about the importance of cultivating the habit of prayer and reading the Bible. Both men were warmly received together as a team—a testimony to their harmonious accord, consistency, and simplicity of presentation when appearing together. The event signaled the unanimity of intent, if not of experience and knowledge, between Bill and Bob.

The Summary of the actual Akron A.A. Program by Frank Amos

It all was covered in seven simple summary statements by Frank Amos to John D. Rockefeller when Amos was sent to Akron to investigate, evaluate, and report back on the Akron program. *DR. BOB and the Good Oldtimers*, pp. 128-136. His briefly presented points were these:

- An alcoholic must realize that he is an alcoholic, incurable from a medical viewpoint, and that he must never drink anything with alcohol in it.
- He must surrender himself absolutely to God, realizing that in himself there is no hope.
- Not only must he want to stop drinking permanently, he must remove from his life other sins such as hatred, adultery, and others which frequently accompany alcoholism. Unless he will do this absolutely, Smith and his associates refuse to work with him.
- He must have devotions every morning–a "quiet time" of prayer and some reading from the Bible and other religious literature. Unless this is faithfully followed, there is grave danger of backsliding.
- He must be willing to help other alcoholics get straightened out. This throws up a protective barrier and strengthens his own willpower and convictions.
- It is important, but not vital, that he meet frequently with other reformed alcoholics and form both a social and a religious comradeship.
- Important, but not vital, that he attend some religious service at least once weekly.

This simple program enabled the first three AAs and most AAs for a decade thereafter to state that, in Akron, they had a 75% success rate among medically incurable alcoholics who really tried; and, soon, in Cleveland, there was a 93% success rate. Those who succeeded not only were cured but widely publicized their own statements that God had cured them of alcoholism. See Richard K. *Early A.A. – Separating Fact From Fiction: How Revisionists Have Lead Our History Astray* (Haverhill, MA: Golden Text Publishing Co., 2003); *New Freedom: Reclaiming Alcoholics Anonymous.* (MA: Golden Text Publishing Co.,

2005). For a detailed picture of this Akron program as I have been able to piece it together after 18 years of research, see *DR. BOB and the Good Oldtimers* (NY: Alcoholics Anonymous World Services, 1980); Dick B., *The First Nationwide A.A. History Conference*; *When Early AAs Were Cured; The James Club and the Original A.A. Program's Absolute Essentials; Real Twelve Step Fellowship History*; and Three Oldtimer Clarence Snyder Sponsees, *Our Legacy to the Faith Community*.

Part Four: The Works Publishing Company Program that Bill Wilson Fashioned, Penned, and Embodied in A.A.'s Big Book

The practice and vice of categorizing A.A. without specifying which A.A.: Well-meaning people have made lots of different and varied attempts to describe the program of Alcoholics Anonymous, interchangeably using language that took no account of the era being described. Some have called A.A. a Christian Fellowship. Dr. Bob did. And it was—if one is talking about the Akron program founded in 1935 and developed through 1938. Some have called A.A. a part of the Oxford Group. But it was never an actual "part" of the Oxford Group either in Akron or on the East Coast. You could fairly say, however, that A.A. as a Society certainly got its start from its Oxford Group associations though its purpose, practices, meetings, and literature were not Oxford Group. Some have said A.A. is a religion. See Charles Bufe. *Alcoholics Anonymous: Cult or Cure?* 2d ed (AZ: See Sharp Press). And it certainly is. It has been ruled to be just that by the courts that have considered the question. Stanton Peele and Charles Bufe. *Resisting Twelve Step Coercion* (AZ: See Sharp Press, 2000). However, the significant question is not whether A.A. is a religion, but rather what A.A. period, what a particular A.A. characterization refers to, and what kind of religion A.A. was and is. See Mel B. *The Spiritual Roots of the Twelve Step Miracle* (MN: Hazelden, 1991), pp. 127-141. Some have said A.A. is spiritual, but not religious. But, as A.A. historian Mel B. has observed, it is doubtful if anyone in A.A. can define or obtain consensus on the meaning of the phrase "spiritual but not religious." Mel B., *Spiritual Roots*, pp. 4-5.

Some have said you don't need to believe in any deity or power in A.A. More and more the pamphlets pouring out of A.A.'s New York headquarters contain this proposition. One of A.A.'s "Conference Approved" pamphlets was revised in 1992 to say these things to the *Young People and A.A.* (NY: Alcoholics Anonymous World Services, Inc., 1992):

> *Myth*: A.A. is a religious organization.
> *Truth*: Some of us in A.A. do have a strong faith; others have none; many are still searching. But we all share the feeling that our way of doing things didn't work (p. 7)

> [One young AA wrote:] Just one glance at the word God in the Twelve Steps, hanging on the wall like a sacred scroll, made it obvious that I didn't belong in this Fellowship of disappointed souls. Let the old folks find a new family and religion in A.A. to replace the ones they lost (p. 39)

And the statement might well be accurate, as far as it goes, if you are describing many in today's A.A., including those who prefer emphasis on not drinking and going to meetings, and those who insist that A.A. is inclusive, but not exclusive; is a universal recovery program; and contains no sectarian doctrines. But the "no-god" viewpoints do not speak for any of the tens of thousands of believing AAs who are Roman Catholics, Jews, and Born-again Christians, many of whom have crossed my path or frequently written their views to me on the reliability of God and the Bible. See also Psalm 115 for the Bible's own statement on the inefficacy of idols as gods. Therefore, the "any old god" or "not-god" stuff might be acceptable to the A.A. of the atheist, the A.A. of the humanist, the A.A. of the still-angry former church member, and perhaps the A.A. of those who have not yet "come to believe." But the integrity and even the existence of any such description (whether it be an A.A. of "any god," "no god," or "Not-God) depends on which period of A.A. is under discussion, on which AA member is doing the opining, and whether one is speaking of the Big Book program of recovery or simply a mixed fellowship of groups and meetings which are considered autonomous, self-governed, and free to believe or not believe what they choose. But such not-god and no god words bear no resemblance to the words and writings of Bill W. and Dr. Bob. See, for example, Big Book 3rd ed., pp. 181, 191.

Certainly any not-god-ness characterization is at variance with A.A.'s oft-repeated statement that the Big Book program is *about* "establishing a relationship with God." See, for example, *Alcoholics Anonymous*, 3rd ed., pp. 13, 28, 29, 72, 100, 164, 452 [And, except for page 452, the pagination in the 4th edition is the same as the pages cited above].

It's no trick to see that there are severely conflicting views today of and about A.A.: (1) First, perhaps, as a *social movement* (with a life-changing program from the Oxford Group, some New Thought "higher power" as a defense against the first drink, and a self-help support group). (2) Or, as an *evolving religious movement* (branching out in many directions to atheists, gays, lesbians, Buddhists, Hindus, impaired physicians and dentists and lawyers, and many other separate groups of like-minded souls—be they policemen, firemen, accountants, or young hod carriers. As such, the original A.A. program simply hasn't "stayed the course," See Dick B. *Real Twelve Step Fellowship History*. And the tension over which is which causes all manner of confusion, criticism, and hostile entrenchment among those who: (1) Very easily and quickly and clearly see A.A.'s religious origins and early Christian program, and (2) Revisionists who haven't been able to abide the existence of *Yahweh* the Creator in a "universal" movement which joyously and passively allows godless language to creep into its expressions, and welcomes those of faith, no faith, any faith, and self-made religion, not to mention atheists.

Now, let's look at the Big Book—all four editions of it—and focus on its basic text to learn how Bill Wilson actually penned his "precise" suggestions for finding and establishing a relationship with God. That path began with "conversion" as its first tenet. See Bill's letter to Dr. Carl Jung telling the famous psychiatrist that his advice to Rowland Hazard that he might be cured by a "genuine conversion" proved to be "the foundation of such success as Alcoholics Anonymous has since achieved." (*Pass It On*, pp. 382-383). Bill's description of the conversion foundation was clearly religious as Bill pointed out to Jung the further advice from Jung that Rowland Hazard "place himself in a religious atmosphere" which prompted Rowland to join the Oxford Group evangelical movement (to use Bill's words).

And how did all the ensuing variety of thoughts and language as to what Bill Wilson was believing, stating, and instructing (all conflicting, to say the least) come about?

Reasons for conflicting descriptions: One answer would point out that A.A. has had several epochs and has taken several different forms—as we have laid out here. Another is that it began in Akron with roots in United Christian Endeavor, the Bible, and its tiny "alcoholic squadron" that met as a Christian Fellowship. Another is that East Coast A.A. took many of its *later* principles and practices from the Oxford Group; and that the Oxford Group (though Protestant in leadership) embraced many Christian ideas but had no doctrinal definitions of God, sin, or conversion. Another is that the Roman Catholic Church had, on several occasions, expressed objections to the Oxford Group as being an heretical sect whose meetings and ideas were to be avoided. See Clair M. Dinger. *Moral Re-Armament: A Study of Its Technical and Religious Nature in the Light of Catholic Teachings* (Washington, D.C.: The Catholic University of America Press, 1961). Another derives from Bill's urge to promote book sales as widely as he could. Another from a growing desire to attract alcoholics of many faiths and no faith. And, yes, even the devil himself seemed constantly to drive A.A. away from God, Jesus Christ, the Bible, and Christian practices. And a plain disparagement of AAs' original freedom to look at their society's religious and Biblical sources and precepts and then be allowed to pursue what their own Big Book described: "**Each individual, in the personal stories, describes in his own language and from his own point of view the way he established his relationship with God**" (Big Book, 4th ed., p. 29). In summary, you *cannot* reconcile these varied convictions without explaining first the variations in A.A. origins, principles, practices, objectives, eras, and influences, and then proclaiming your self-assumed ability to make them all fit one mold. A task no less difficult than that of forming a single-minded Iraqi democracy composed of ethnically cleansed champions of religious freedom.

The Persisting Pre-eminence of A.A. Alcoholics Anonymous has, over the years, published and distributed some forty million copies of its Big Book. It has hovered around a world-wide membership of two million. It has spawned over two hundred similar Twelve Step programs; and it has been the darling of insurance companies, treatment programs, therapies, courts, correctional officers, and even government entities for at least fifty years. The emergent program in the basic text – encompassing the writing of the Twelve Steps, the publication of the Big Book and later editions in and after 1939, followed by the more and more rigid and doctrinal meeting restrictions and conference formats of later years – warrants and will receive attention here. The discussion will outline the ensuing development of the "for profit corporation" (Works Publishing Company) formed by

Bill Wilson and his business partner Hank Parkhurst and the sale of stock to Dr. Silkworth, Charles Towns, and AAs themselves. See Mitchel, *Silkworth*, pp. 64-69. This corporation published a basic text written almost entirely by Bill Wilson, with accompanying personal stories largely written by or for other individual AAs, and whose Twelve Step recovery program came to be recognized as *the* A.A. Program of today—however it may be understood or misunderstood.

The Big Book turnabout of 1939: Bill Wilson was a bargainer, a compromiser, and a promoter. He returned to Akron in 1938 when Akron's spiritual program had earned its spurs. He there proposed writing a book that would enable the A.A. program and its message to be passed along to others. He met with stiff opposition, winning his point in an election held by the members, and which gave him only a two-vote majority.

Members favored the Book of James in the Bible, wanted to have their fellowship called "The James Club," and were told their fellowship and book would be called "The James Club," only to learn that Bill and Bob decided finally that the Society and the Book were both given the name "Alcoholics Anonymous." See Dick B., *The James Club*, pp. 2-6; *DR. BOB*, pp. 71, 213; Mitchel, *Silkworth*, p. 65; *Pass It On*, p. 147. Pioneer members, primarily those in Akron, had achieved their success with the simple seven-point program reported out by Frank Amos. Yet Bill wrote a basic text that scarcely gave a nod to the original program. Early Akron A.A. had developed and conducted a Christian Fellowship which took its basic ideas from the Bible; relied on the Creator; accepted Jesus Christ; stressed elimination of sin, growth in fellowship through Bible study, prayer, and morning meditation; and witnessing to the newcomer. But virtually every trace of these factors was lost, removed, or destroyed in the writing and publication of Bill's book. Instead, Bill finally posited that there were six "word of mouth" steps which in no way resembled the Akron program. See Dick B., *The Conversion of Bill W.*, pp. 181-183. These he nonetheless "expanded" to twelve with the assertion that he had eliminated the "wiggle room" inherent in the alleged six. Then he boldly passed along to future readers the idea that "these were the steps we took which are suggested as a program of recovery." But they weren't!

Bill's own forte and focus: Bill himself was far more conversant with the Oxford Group and its ideas than with Bible and Christian precepts. He said so to A.A. founders T. Henry and Clarace Williams in a recorded talk with them in 1954. Dick B. *The Akron Genesis*, 2d ed., 1998, p. 136. One biographer observed. "Catholicism fascinated him. His spiritual adviser, Father Ed Dowling, was a devout Roman Catholic, and although Bill had stopped going to church in a formal way when he left the Congregational Church of his boyhood, he had become a Christian without a church." Cheever. *My Name is Bill*, p. 201. As early as 1934, Bill became very active in the Oxford Group. See Dick B., *New Light on Alcoholism*. Shoemaker's personal journals reveal that Bill was given substantial responsibility in 1935 for a major Oxford Group event which brought Carl Hambro, President of the League of Nations, to the United States on an Oxford Group tour. Also, Bill and his wife attended a great many Oxford Group meetings, went to several house-parties, and (as Lois recorded in her diaries) met a number of Oxford Group leaders and activists including Frank Buchman, Charles Haines, Irving Harris, Cleve Hicks, Garth Lean, Jim Newton, and Sam Shoemaker. Bill belonged to the Oxford Group businessman's team. Finally, the Wilsons left the Group in August of 1937, alleging that the Group had taught AAs more about what not to do than what to do. Strangely, however, Bill turned around in 1939 and then based all the major ideas of the Big Book on the Oxford Group's life-changing principles and practices without, for many many years, ever giving any indication that this is what he had done. See *The Language of the Heart*, pp. 200-202, 296-298; *Pass It On*, pp. 173-174, 199. Mitchel, *Silkworth*, p. 65.

As Bill approached the actual writing of the Big Book, he spent long periods with an American Oxford Group leader, the Reverend Sam Shoemaker, Jr., rector of the Calvary Episcopal Church in New York. They discussed the principles of recovery as Shoemaker and Bill saw them. And Bill asked Sam to write the Twelve Steps—something that Sam declined to do. This bit of historical eye-witness evidence has simply not been reported by any historian I know of, other than myself. And see also Irving Harris, *The Breeze of the Spirit*. NY: The Seabury Press, 1978; Bill Pittman and Dick B. *Courage to Change: The Christian Roots of the Twelve Step Movement* (MN: Hazelden, 1994); Dick B. *The Conversion of Bill W.*, pp. 202-203; *New Light on Alcoholism: God, Sam Shoemaker, and A.A.*, 2d ed., 1999.

But the upshot of the Big Book program as first published is that its text called upon, involved, and yet modified, the books and language of many different persons, writings, and entities: Dr. Carl Jung, Professor William James, Dr. William Silkworth, lay therapist Richard Peabody, the Bible, the teachings of Rev. Sam Shoemaker and Anne Smith, the twenty-eight life-changing principles and practices of the Oxford Group, Quiet Time, a variety of religious writings, and New Thought Movement jargon. Dick B. *The First Nationwide A.A. History Conference*, pp. 33, 37-39; *The Conversion of Bill W.*, pp. 77-110, 171-174.

Therefore, when you study the Big Book and want to understand its sources and meanings, you should equip yourself with a review of all fourteen or more well-springs of its ideas. See Dick B. *A New Way Out: New Path—Familiar Road Signs—Our Creator's Guidance* (Kihei, HI: Paradise Research Publications, Inc., 2006); *The Good Book-Big Book Guidebook: How to Include the Creator's Impact on Early A.A. in Recovery Programs Today* (Kihei, HI: Paradise Research Publications, 2006). And, when you study the Twelve Steps and want to understand their specific, individual sources and meanings, you would do well to start with the immense influence that the books, articles, sermons, and language of Sam Shoemaker had on the ultimate language of each Step. See Dick B., *Twelve Steps for You.* (Kihei, HI: Paradise Research Publications, 2006).

At last it is time to review the Sam Shoemaker picture in light of his contribution to A.A. ideas and his specific influence on the language of the Twelve Steps. As Bill Wilson said, in a variety of ways, without Shoemaker there would have been no A.A. For it was on the solid foundation of Shoemaker's teachings that Bill finally framed and built his own Twelve Steps of recovery.

The Sam Shoemaker Reservoir and Basic Contributions

You cannot fairly appraise Sam Shoemaker's legacy to A.A. without knowing the depth and breadth of what Sam had to offer. Sam wrote over thirty books, at least half of which were circulating (before A.A.'s 12 Steps and Big Book were published in 1939) and being circulated in New York, Akron, and the Oxford Group. See Dick B. *Making Known the Biblical History and Roots of Alcoholics Anonymous,* (Kihei, HI: Paradise Research Publications, 2005).

Sam was also a prolific writer of sermons, pamphlets, and articles for the Calvary Evangel, his parish newsletter. The sermons and articles included his 1935 piece on "The Way to Find God." Also, his pamphlet on "A First Century Christian Fellowship" (the name by which the Oxford Group was known during A.A.'s formative years, and a name which Dr. Bob perhaps used to characterize Akron A.A. itself). Sam also wrote "Three Levels of Life," and "What if I Had but One Sermon to Preach" (two pamphlets which were tucked into the back of Anne Smith's Journal). Sam's booklet "One Boy's Influence" was quoted in Anne Smith's Journal. Six other Shoemaker books are known for sure to have been owned, and read by, Dr. Bob and his wife Anne Smith. In all, therefore, Sam's ideas reached A.A. through his books; his pamphlets; his published sermons; his *Evangel* articles; his personal conversations with Bill; his influence on Bill's mentors Reverend Irving Harris, Julia Harris, Rowland Hazard, Shep Cornell, Hanford Twitchell, Victor Kitchen, and others; and Sam's actual conduct of, and leadership in, the very first alcoholic meetings on the East Coast. These meetings were actually Oxford Group assemblages. Sam's ideas were also passed down the chute via Calvary Rescue Mission, where Bill first went for help and where he later went to find and help other drunks. To boot, it is not surprising that Shoemaker was listed among the ten most famous preachers in America and had been awarded D.D. and S.T.D. honorary degrees.

Shoemaker ideas can be found in the very language of the Twelve Steps. They can be found almost verbatim in the Big Book. They are part of A.A. fellowship jargon. And they were later reiterated and explained when Shoemaker addressed A.A. International Conventions in St. Louis and subsequently at Long Beach. See Dick B., *New Light on Alcoholism,* 2d ed., pp. 327-330 (as to St. Louis, with reference to the complete text in A.A. literature) and pp. 330-335 (as to Long Beach). Also in the articles he wrote for A.A.'s *Grapevine.* (*New Light,* pp. 335-345). Also when he wrote about A.A., as he frequently did, in his own later books and pamphlets (*New Light*, pp. 345-354). Recall too that Sam's colleagues described him as a "Bible Christian." His books, sermons, and articles were permeated with references to the very Bible verses and chapters that became the foundation of A.A.'s own basic ideas. Principles that were studied in, and borrowed from, the Bible itself by A.A.'s Akron pioneers. Additional Shoemaker input came from Sam's frequent references to the writings of Professor William James, whom Bill Wilson was later to call a "founder" of A.A. and from whose *The Varieties of Religious Experiences*, Bill obtained some significant principles. Furthermore, Sam was an outspoken advocate of Quiet Time, Bible study, prayer, and the use of devotionals; and these practices became part and parcel of early A.A. meetings, group quiet times, and personal prayer life.

Shoemaker/Wilson correspondence located at the Episcopal Church Archives in Austin, Texas also demonstrates the degree to which Wilson confided in Sam from the beginning of their friendship. See Dick B., *New Light on Alcoholism* for materials unearthed there.

Specific Shoemaker Ideas in A.A.

Every AA who stays in our fellowship long enough to be exposed to its Big Book, its Twelve Steps, and its meeting buzzwords will readily recognize on sight the following thoughts that seem to have come directly from the books and other writings of Sam Shoemaker.

These include: (1) Self-surrender. (2) Self is not God. (3) God either is, or He isn't. (4) "Turning point." (5) Conversion. (6) Prayer. (7) Fellowship. (8) Willingness. (9) Self-examination. (10) Confession of faults to God, self, and another. (11) Amends. (12) "Thy will be done." (13) Spiritual Experience. (14) Spiritual Awakening. (15) The unmanageable life. (16) Power greater than ourselves. (17) God as you understand Him. (18) The "Four Absolutes"-- honesty, purity, unselfishness, and love. (19) Guidance of God. (20) "Faith without works is dead." (21) "Love thy neighbor as thyself." (22) Clear references to Almighty God (using Bible terms) as our "Creator," "Maker," "Father," "Spirit,"

"God of our fathers," and "Father of Lights." (23) The Lord's Prayer. (24) Jesus' "sermon on the mount." (25) Self-centeredness. (26) Fear. (27) Grudges. (28) Quiet Time. (29) Reliance on God. (30) Relationship with God. (31) "Giving it away to keep it." (32) "News, not views." (33) God has a plan. (34) Seeking God first. (35) Belief in God. (36) Born again. (37) Marvel at what God has done for you. (38) Let go! (39) Abandon yourself to Him [God]. (40) "Not my will but Thine be done." And many others.

You can find, in my title *New Light on Alcoholism: God, Sam Shoemaker, and A.A.* 2d ed., pp. 150-172, a list of 149 Shoemaker expressions that very closely parallel A.A. language. Many more can be found in specific quotations from Shoemaker's books, books which have been fully reviewed in my *New Light* work on Shoemaker.

Shoemaker and our Twelve Steps

There are many Step sources: Make no mistake. Whatever Bill Wilson may have said or implied from time to time, Sam Shoemaker was not the only source of A.A.'s spiritual ideas. Wilson often steered his applause in Sam's direction and away from its Oxford Group source in an effort to avoid Roman Catholic and other objections to the Oxford Group from which A.A.'s ideas also came and out of which early A.A. had sprung. Moreover, Bill never mentioned A.A. specifics from Dr. Bob, Anne Smith, the Bible, Quiet Time, Dr. Carl Jung, Professor William James, Dr. William D. Silkworth, Richard Peabody, New Thought writers, God's direct guidance, or the huge amount of Christian literature that was daily fare in early A.A.

The Akron difference: Remember also! Dr. Bob said he did not write the Twelve Steps and had nothing to do with writing them. Those Steps represented Bill's personal and variant interpretation of the spiritual program that had been in progress since 1935. Dr. Bob emphasized, on more than one occasion, that A.A.'s basic ideas had come from study of the Bible. Dick B., *The Akron Genesis.* And Bill never disagreed with the statement; therefore the statement stands as authority for the Biblical origins of A.A. First of all, Dr. Bob studied the Bible for two and a half years and then nightly. Daily for three months in 1935, Anne Smith read the Bible to Bill and Bob. Dr. Bob regularly read the Bible to AAs themselves. He quoted the Bible to AAs. He gave them Bible literature. And he frequently stressed Bible study, stating that the Book of James, 1 Corinthians 13, and Jesus' sermon on the mount (Matthew 5 to 7) were considered absolutely essential in the early spiritual recovery program. Bill Wilson and Dr. Bob both said that the sermon on the mount contained the underlying philosophy of A.A. These are facts, not just the naïve prating of some Bible-thumper. Dick B. *Dr. Bob and His Library; Anne Smith's Journal; The James Club and The Original A.A. Program's Absolute Essentials; When Early AAs Were Cured and Why; The Good Book and The Big Book; The Good Book-Big Book Guidebook; That Amazing Grace; The Akron Genesis of Alcoholics Anonymous; Real Twelve Step Fellowship History; Twelve Steps for You.*

Sam's specific imprint on each Step: Sam's own imprint is on the Twelve Steps–Steps that were fabricated entirely at the hand of Bill Wilson. Every one of them. Sam Shoemaker's imprint was on the presentation of Oxford Group ideas that Ebby Thacher made to Bill Wilson in Towns Hospital. You can see that even today if you look at the last seven or eight pages of Bill's Story in Chapter One of the Big Book. And now we will briefly take a look at just where Shoemaker's language parallels the language in each of the Twelve Steps. All these parallels are meticulously documented with citations to Shoemaker works and A.A. literature. See my title, *New Light on Alcoholism: God, Sam Shoemaker, and A.A.*

Step One: Shoemaker spoke of the gap between man and God which man is powerless to bridge, man having lost the power to deal with sin for himself. As to the alcoholic's unmanageable life, Sam referred to the prayer in the Oxford Group so often described in "Victor's Story" which was also quoted by Anne Smith in her journal: "God manage me, because I can't manage myself."

Step Two: Sam spelled out the need for a power greater than ourselves. He quoted Hebrews 11:6 for the proposition that God is. He declared: God is God, and self is not God; and man must so believe. Sam urged, from Matthew 6:33, seeking God first. He espoused an "experiment of faith" by which man "acts as if," believing that God is; seeks God first in his actions, does God's will, and then knows God by seeing that God provides the needed power. In support of this idea, Sam frequently cited John 7:17, which A.J. Russell said in *For Sinners Only* was Sam's favorite verse.

Step Three: Sam taught about the crisis of self-surrender as the turning point for a religious life, quoting William James' *The Varieties of Religious Experience.* You can find this language in Sam's first significant title (*Realizing Religion*, published in 1921). Sam said the surrender of self results in being born again; and Sam declared that man must make a decision to renounce sins, accept Jesus Christ as Saviour; and begin Christian life in earnest. Sam illustrated a typical surrender, using language similar to that in A.A.: namely, a "decision to cast my will and my life on God." Many times, Sam said one need only surrender as much of himself as he understands to as much of God as he understands. A clear precursor of A.A.'s "God as we understood Him"–which has unfortunately been misunderstood and has been attributed to other sources.

Step Four: Sam wrote of conducting a self examination to find where one's life fell short of the Four Absolute Standards of Jesus: honesty, purity, unselfishness, and love. One was to write down exactly where he had "fallen short." (Matthew 7:1-5). There was to be, to use Anne Smith's language, a "moral test." And then there was a "moral obligation" to face these facts, recognize these as blocks to God, and be "ruthlessly, realistically honest" in the process.

Step Five: Shoemaker said there must be honesty with self and honesty with God, quoted James 5:16 for the importance of honest confession to others, and stressed the need for detailed sharing of secrets.

Step Six: Though the fact of Bill's borrowing of this "conviction" step from the Oxford Group 5 C's seems to have been overlooked, Shoemaker taught often about the need for man's conviction that he has been miserable, has (by his sins) become estranged from God, and needs to come back to God in honest penitence. (The "Five C's" were Confidence, Confession, Conviction, Conversion, and Continuance). Sam urged willingness to ask God exactly where one was failing and then to admit that sin.

Step Seven: Sam clarified the "conversion" step of the Oxford Group's 5 C's and discussed Step Seven in that light. It meant a new birth, he said. It meant humility. It meant, for Shoemaker, the assumption upon ourselves of God's will for us and the opening of ourselves to receiving the "grace of God which alone converts." It meant "drawing near and putting ourselves in position to be converted. . . utter dedication to the will of God," he wrote. Shoemaker often defined "'sin' as that which blocks us from God and from others." So, originally, did Big Book language. "Sin" was mentioned specifically in the original Steps. And the "blocks" and "obstacles" can be found mentioned in Big Book language. Furthermore, the totality of all the life-changing steps hangs on early A.A.'s definition of sin and the "removal" process of examining for sin, confessing sin, becoming convicted of sin, and becoming converted through surrendering and being cleansed of sin nature by the power of God. The conversion experience, according to Shoemaker and early A.A., established or enabled rediscovery of a "relationship with God" and initiated the new life that developed from that relationship with God which conversion opened. Since both of Wilson's Sixth and Seventh Steps were new to A.A. thinking and both added something to the original "surrenders" to Jesus Christ, these Steps cannot easily be understood without considering them in the light of a complete surrender (Matthew 6:10; 7:21-24), a new birth (John 3:1-8; Galatians 4:1-7), a new relationship (John 14:6,1 John 3:1-2), and a release from sin (James 5:15; 1 Peter 2:24), as Shoemaker saw the process and as Bill attempted to write it into the recovery path.

Step Eight: Wilson added this step to the Oxford Group's "restitution" practice. Bill also incorporated the Shoemaker talk of "willingness"—the willingness to ask God's help in removing the blocks, having been convicted of the need for restitution, and then being sent "to someone with restoration and apology." (Matthew 5:25).

Step Nine: Sam said the last stand of self is pride. There can be no talk of humility, he said, until pride licks the dust, and one then acts to make full restoration and restitution for wrongs done. In support, Sam quoted from the sermon on the mount those verses enjoining the bringing of a gift to the altar without first being reconciled to one's brother (Matthew 5:22-24). These verses were often quoted in Akron A.A. Restitution was not merely a good deed to be done. It was a command of God from the Bible that wrongs be righted as part of the practicing the principle of love. If one understands Shoemaker, one can understand the absurdity of some present-day AAs' guilt-ridden suggestions about writing a letter to a dead person or volunteering help for the down-trodden or making a substitute gift to some worthy cause. These acts may be appealing, but Sam taught that the required amends were not about works. They were about love and restorative acts!

Step Ten: This step concerned *daily* surrender and the Oxford Group idea of "continuance." Sam taught that it was necessary to continue self-examination, confession, conviction, the seeking of God's help, and the prompt making of amends. This continued action was to follow the new relationship with God and others that resulted from removal of the sin problem in the earlier steps.

Step Eleven: Sam wrote eloquently about Quiet Time, Bible study, prayer, and "meditation" (reading the "Word" and "listening" for God's guidance). Sam urged daily contact with God for guidance, forgiveness, strength, and spiritual growth. So does A.A.'s Big Book. Quiet Time was a "must" in early A.A. And Shoemaker meticulously defined every aspect of a Quiet Time–from the necessity for beginning after a new birth, to a new willingness to study, pray, listen, and read rather than to speak first and lead with the chin.

Step Twelve: This step comprehends: (1) A spiritual awakening, the exact meaning of which Shoemaker spelled out in his books and in his talks to AAs. He said a spiritual awakening consists of conversion, prayer, fellowship, and witness. (2) A message about what God has accomplished for us, a phrase which Shoemaker himself used, saying, in several ways: "You have to give

Christianity away to keep it;" and he said this quite often. (3) Practicing the new way of living in harmony with God's will and with love toward others, an idea easily recognized from Sam's teachings that a spiritual awakening comes from conversion, that the gospel message concerns God's grace and power, and that the principles to be practiced are defined in the Bible.

Accordingly, our Twelfth Step language, studied *without* knowledge of its Shoemaker roots, becomes ill-defined and illusory, and subject to endless, mindless, alkie interpretations. A.A. Big Book students know that none of the foregoing three Twelfth Step ideas wound up being fleshed out of the words as set forth or explained in the chapter of the Big Book dealing with the Twelfth Step. To be frank, A.A.'s Big Book left Christianity in the dust at that point. In so doing, AAs lost an understanding of what Sam Shoemaker taught and Dr. Bob emphasized: Conversion was a necessity. The gospel message was carrying the good news of its availability and implementation. Love and service were empowered and became obligatory as defined in the Book of Acts, the Four Absolutes, 1 Corinthians 13, Jesus' Sermon on the Mount, the Book of James, and other specific parts of the Bible. AAs looked to the Bible for the principles to be practiced.

The Big Book Backdrop

Before we leave Sam Shoemaker and the Big Book itself, let's consider some features that have been given little or no credit by those teaching Big Book ideas, workshops, and seminars.

Wilson's conversion quest and experience: The root of Bill Wilson's recovery thinking was conversion, conversion, conversion. Dick B. *The Conversion of Bill W.,* 2006.

Bill's grandfather had been converted and never drank for the rest of his life. Ebby had been converted at Calvary Mission and told Bill about it. Bill was converted at the altar at Calvary Rescue Mission. Bill had been told by Dr. Silkworth that he could be cured by Jesus Christ the Great Physician. Carl Jung had opined that "conversion" could be a cure for alcoholism. William James wrote about many "conversion" healings and cures—all "varieties". Bill went from the Mission to Towns Hospital, said he'd seek the help of the Great Physician, called out to God, had his "hot flash" conversion experience, and never drank again. He validated that "conversion" experience by reading in Professor William James's treatise about the many conversion experiences where alcoholics were cured in Mission services. Silkworth and Bill's wife believed, with Bill, that Bill had experienced a very real conversion.

This original "conversion" solution became the very foundation of Bill's original ideas about how to recover through the power of God and be able to say, as he did, that the Lord had cured him!

As we will see, Bill did not pretend to a theological understanding of "conversion." He just heard about it (from his grandpa's experience). He just learned about it (from Dr. Silkworth's explanations of the Great Physician). He just saw it (as Ebby Thacher stood before him and boldly proclaimed his conversion at Calvary Rescue Mission). He just "experienced" it (as he himself made his decision for Christ at the Calvary Mission altar). He employed it (in his decision at Towns Hospital to call on the Great Physician for help). He benefited from it at Towns Hospital in his "hot flash" experience (closely resembling in Bill's description the very experience his grandfather had had years before) and was cured of alcoholism (as he himself declared in the Big Book account on page 191). He just assured himself of the facts as his physician and his wife both confirmed that he had experienced a "genuine conversion"—just like that prescribed by Dr. Carl Jung. And he certainly validated it for himself by reading countless cases of and descriptions of such conversions as he devoured the William James book that very day (William James, *The Varieties of Religious Experience*. NY: First Vintage Books/The Library of America Edition, 1990), pp. 66-72, 93-97, 107-108, 114-116, 146-154, 162-176, 177-200, 201-228, 266-304, 348, 414-431, 448-463.

I prefer to look at "conversion" as Bill Wilson probably viewed it and as it was explained to him by William James and Sam Shoemaker. Bill got the "solution" of "conversion" (as one writer who drew the wrong conclusion about William James and conversion said:) "Bill Wilson linked James's portrayal of 'conversion' with what he had learned—directly from Dr. Silkworth and indirectly via Rowland and Ebby, from Dr. Jung. . . ." See Richard M. Dubiel. *The Road to Fellowship* (NY: iUniverse, Inc., 2004), p. 160, n. 175. And why the revisionists, amateur theologians, and historians didn't let it go at that may remain forever a mystery. They should have let the facts speak for themselves, just as I have tried to let them speak above.

Instead of telling us about the good old-time religion of Billy Sunday and the Evangelist healers—as very probably seen by both Wilson and Smith—these well-intentioned folk have tried to turn the Bill Wilson story into a mythical program for removing ourselves from God Almighty. They've analyzed and promoted every conceivable kind of supposed historical rooting that connected up with "mind-cure," the "Emanuel Movement," the Washingtonians, Courtney Baylor, Richard Peabody, New Thought writers, humanists, illusory "spirituality," "higher powers," and cosmic nonsense.

Where on earth can you find such stuff in the Bible—which Dr. Bob said contained the basic ideas of A.A.? Where in the Christian Endeavor movement and Congregational Church in which Dr. Bob was raised? Where on earth can you find not gods in the tiny village and East Congregational Church of East Dorset, Vermont—where Bill Wilson got a lot heavier dose of Christian conversion than has ever been reported! All to the good if you concede that even Bill Wilson later picked up on some of the nonsensical language of so-called "spirituality." And then talked about his hostility to religion in the manner of an angry drunk addressing bar room friends. All to the bad if you ignore the solution to alcoholism in the simple form in which Bill Wilson originally tried to sell it. There is no evidence that Wilson went to a Bible, to a dictionary, to a theological treatise, or to a rabbi or minister or priest to find out what his grandpa, Carl Jung, Rowland Hazard, and the Rescue Missions meant when they talked of "conversion." It seems that Wilson didn't try to explain it. For many years, he just adopted it—on the authority of grandpa, of the Bible, of revivals, Silkworth, and the Missions without ever trying to reconcile the predispositions of Jung, James, and Emmet Fox.

Shoemaker's "Act as if": Appealing to atheists, agnostics, and unbelievers, Bill picked up from Sam Shoemaker's writings and emphasis on John 7:17 the proposition found in the Twelve Step "practical program of action" that, if one tried an experiment of faith – as Sam described it – and did God's will, that person would find and know God as an experience—a religious or spiritual experience. And this, of course, would produce the "solution" which was deemed so vital to Bill and expressed in the Big Book's second chapter.

Additional ideas borrowed from others: Bill himself said in a *Grapevine* article years after writing his Big Book that he got all the ideas for the Steps from Silkworth, James, and the teachings of Sam. But traces of New Thought language had crept into the Big Book and Step approaches. Richard Peabody's "no cure for alcoholism" theory had crept into Step Ten language despite statements by all the founders that the Lord had "cured" them of alcoholism. Although the original Big Book materials had contained Biblical and Christian materials, and lessons from the Rescue Missions, these were all tossed out in an attempt to universalize A.A. appeal and secularize its membership. While many Bible ideas—even a few quotations—remained in the Big Book, unacknowledged and without citation, the Bible as a recognized source simply went unmentioned.

See Dick B., *The Conversion of Bill W., Real Twelve Step Fellowship History, The James Club, When Early AAs Were Cured and Why, and The Good Book-Big Book Guidebook.*

Part Five: The Reshaping of the Big Book Program Beginning in 1939 Just After its Publication and Before Bill began suffering for more than a decade from Deep Depressions, while others stepped in with several of their own Interpretive Programs and Thoughts

Bill Wilson suffered from deep depressions all of his life. They began in his youth with the separation of his parents and soon the untimely death of his first love. They continued through his drinking years. And they became all but totally disabling beginning in 1942 and continuing through the year 1955. The situation is no secret. It is covered in A.A.'s *Pass It On.* It is discussed in detail by Mel B. in his *My Search for Bill W.* (MN: Hazelden, 2000), pp. 22, 23, 34, 36, 38, 39, 44, 58, 115, and 117. Recent Wilson biographies have given it even further play. It is also covered in my recent title *The Conversion of Bill W.*

The sad impact of Bill's lengthy period of depression and incapacity is that, during that period of his illness, A.A. began to change dramatically—sometimes for the better and sometimes for the worse—almost the moment Bill published the Big Book in the Spring of 1939. The events transpired as follows.

Detours from the Big Book's Specific Path to Recovery

Bill's Big Book basic text, in its last two editions, has consisted of some 164 text pages. Their stated purpose was to show others precisely how an alleged 100 men had women had recovered. In the middle of the Big Book text, Bill added, however, that the real purpose of the book was to help alcoholics to find a "power greater than themselves" that would solve all their problems. While the two objectives were not congruous, the various early segments of the book—Bill's story, the solution, more about alcoholism, and then the chapter for the agnostics—were a prelude to Bill's suggestions as to how one could change his life through a conversion—often called a religious experience, later a spiritual experience, still later a spiritual awakening, and finally a personality change sufficient to overcome alcoholism.

But Bill's path, as laid out in his text, was not the path that had been taken so successfully in Bill's own conversion at the Mission, or in the "real surrenders" of the earlier Akron fellowship. Nor was his path followed in any but a general way by the spin-off groups that began appearing in 1939. A former Indiana professor Glenn F. Chesnut has done extensive and carefully presented writing through his Hindsfoot Foundation on many of the people and writings discussed below. For example, on Richmond Walker, Father Ralph Pfau, Ed Webster, the AA of Akron pamphlets, and other spin-off works of the 1940's. While some of his own comments can be considered controversial, I commend his website and works to those who want further easily read documentation and important references. See Hindsfoot Foundation. http://hindsfoot.org/tabcont.html. In my judgment, his writing and research approximate the kind that would have prevented much of the historical distortion in A.A. by those who simply didn't research or report all of the facts. Other examples of today's encouraging historical environment and meticulous documentation are the works of Richard K. (on A.A. successes, cures, and historical errors); Dale Mitchel (on Dr. Silkworth's emphasis on the Great Physician and Jesus Christ), William G. Borchert (who seems to have had access to valuable historical papers and records of Lois Wilson), Mary Darrah (who stands out as one of the earliest really to see the Akron story for what it is), Rev. Howard Clinebell, Ph.D. (whose early investigation of A.A. and recently published pastoral counseling work provide important descriptions and judgments on A.A. itself, the Salvation Army, the Missions, the YMCA, and other contributing sources), Bill Pittman (who seemed always to have a real understanding of the total A.A. picture tucked away in his vest for occasional enlightenment), Mitchell K., (who spent years placing the full Clarence Snyder and Cleveland stories for the world to see); the three anonymous old-timer sponsees of Clarence Snyder (who have preserved in the conduct of their retreats and in their Legacy book the heart of Clarence's teachings), and Mel B. (an accomplished writer with long-term sobriety who has observed A.A. history in progress, substantially contributed to *Pass It On*, and swooped onto the history scene many times with various helpful sidelights and biographical portraits.). Some of the earlier writers seemed determined to change the face of A.A.

and appeared unwilling to research, adequately describe, or accurately report the entire picture. And, in my own judgment, the remark of the recently deceased Oxford Group activist and my friend, James Houck (who got sober in 1934 just before Bill Wilson, and spent his later years spreading the Oxford Group principles and practices around today's AAs) offers the greatest present-day challenge to history writers, readers, researchers, and students. Jim wrote in his endorsement of one of my titles: "Take God out of A.A., and you have nothing." The remark particularly applies to those who still write A.A. materials side-stepping every part of A.A. which originally involved God, Jesus Christ, and prayer. Sad though their approach has been, there is solace in the fact that you can obscure desired recovery with blackouts, but you can't change facts themselves.

Clarence Snyder and Cleveland A.A. Perhaps the interpretive spin offs started constructively in May, 1939 when Clarence Snyder took the Bible, the Oxford Group Four Absolutes, the Big Book, and the Twelve Steps to Cleveland and made hay with the old and the new, retaining strong ties to both. Cleveland's groups grew from one to thirty in a year. The success rate there soared from the previous 75% in Akron to 93%. And Clarence developed guides to taking the steps and to sponsorship. See Three Clarence Snyder Sponsee Old-timers and Their Wives: *Our A.A. Legacy to the Faith Community: A Twelve-Step Guide for Those Who Want to Believe*. Comp. ed. by Dick B. Winter Park, (FL: Came to Believe Publications, 2005).

Dr. Bob, Sister Ignatia, and St. Thomas Hospital as a special focus agreed upon by Dr. Bob and Bill: In 1940—apparently by express agreement between Bill and Dr. Bob—Akron began to be focused on hospitalization and Twelfth-stepping as part of the work by Dr. Bob and Sister Ignatia at St. Thomas Hospital in Akron. This work retained the important hospitalization of old. But Sister Ignatia did add some new approaches. Among other things, she would hand out to patients a copy of Thomas A Kempis, *The Imitation of Christ;* she would take the men into the sanctuary in connection with their Third Steps; and she would pass out Sacred Heart medallions to them on their completion of hospitalization. Both Dr. Bob and Anne Smith were moving toward their declining years in energy and effort, but Ignatia consulted them both quite often. The Ignatia story is well covered in Mary C. Darrah. *Sister Ignatia: Angel of Alcoholics Anonymous.*

(Chicago: Loyola University Press, 1992); and, while it cannot be said that the A.A. program thereby changed, it does seem that the very brief St. Thomas Hospital stint with both Dr. Bob and Sister Ignatia did (even as it does in treatment programs today) incline St. Thomas patients to believe they had completed their rehabilitation even though Akron Group Number One was still meeting, it was unlikely they were truly free of damage from abuse and untreated alcoholism, and Dr. Bob and Anne were still active and pointing newcomers to the abundant life promised by the Good Book in John 10:10 and 3 John 2.

Father Ed Dowling, S.J., entered the scene in late 1940; he communicated with Bill for the next twenty years. Their subject matter: Bill's "second conversion," his "Fifth Step" with Dowling, Dowling's interest in the Exercises of St. Ignatius, and the steady flow of letters between the two men. See Robert Fitzgerald. *The Soul of Sponsorship: The Friendship of Fr. Ed Dowling, S.J., and Bill Wilson in Letters.* (Hazelden, 1995).

Bill's period of overwhelming depression: About 1942, Bill suffered his deep, severe, almost immobilizing depression which spanned the next thirteen years. It was not his first bout, but certainly was his longest. And still other leaders and programs were, for whatever reason, starting or attempting to, an obvious leadership gap.

Richmond Walker had a spotty past as a recycled drunk. He gained an interest in the Oxford Group and its literature as early as 1934. He joined the Oxford Group in 1939 to get sober, but didn't stay sober for much over two years. However, he gained extensive knowledge of Oxford Group ideas. In May of 1942, he entered A.A. and was involved in three very influential literary works. He started with a devotional titled *God Calling*, written by two women and edited by Oxford Group writer A.A. Russell. In 1945, a Massachusetts A.A group published Walker's *For Drunks Only* which was filled with Oxford Group ideas, A.A. principles, and sobriety suggestions. He offered it to A.A. for publication and was declined. In 1948, Walker worked with *God Calling* and converted it to a recovery devotional that has sold in the millions, though also declined by A.A. itself. That devotional is titled *Twenty-Four Hours Book.*

Father Ralph Pfau: Father Pfau was the first Roman Catholic priest to get sober in Alcoholics Anonymous (he came in on November 10, 1943). Using the pen name Father John Doe, he wrote fourteen *Golden Books* back in the 1940's and 50's and early 60's. They are still being read and used by A.A.'s today. Then Pfau changed from pamphlet writing to three much longer books, including *Sobriety and Beyond* (1955).

Ed Webster: In 1946, in Minneapolis, Ed Webster published *The Little Red Book* under the sponsorship of the A.A. Nicollet Group. Its title was "An Interpretation of the Twelve Steps." Ed had the help and support of Dr. Bob, who gave numerous suggestions for wording various passages. It was adapted widely by other groups. Ed also wrote *Stools and Bottles* (1955), *Barroom Reveries* (1958) and *Our Devilish Alcoholic Personalities* (in 1970, just a year before his death).

Other supplemental ideas and writings at the local level: The foregoing six spin-offs were certainly not the only ones. All over the United States, local groups began publishing their own guides and pamphlets. See Wally P. *But, For The Grace of God: How Intergroups & Central Offices Carried the Message of Alcoholics Anonymous in the 1940's*. (WV: The Bishop of Books, 1995).

Bill's *Twelve Steps and Twelve Traditions*: By the time Bill Wilson had finally pulled out of his depression, Anne Smith was dead. Dr. Bob was dead. Bill had set about writing a whole new interpretive essay of his own in *Twelve Steps and Twelve Traditions*. It was meticulously edited by two Roman Catholic Jesuit priests.

Recovery Literature: In later years, recovery centers and treatment literature substantially pre-empted the publication and distribution of instructional literature. And, as all the foregoing developments occurred, the A.A. success rates became observably more and more dismal—dropping from its original rate of at least 75% to its present rate of about 5%. For some of the plentiful documentation, see Richard K. *New Freedom: Reclaiming Alcoholics Anonymous*. Yet, even though they attend meetings where newcomers disappear, relapses are evident, and old-timers cannot be found, there are those who want to quibble about statistics, successes, and relapses. They insist that A.A. works. They blame the lack of singleness of purpose. They blame compulsory attendance. They blame religion. They blame rational recovery. And they seldom present a word about documented and recently developed history. But what forty dedicated AAs did in the 1930's stands in stark contrast to what scientists are noting, statistics are revealing, and government-funded grants are enabling. That is that, at best, present-day A.A. is doing little better than other recovery programs—whether they be Christian, "rational," treatment, rehab, therapy, pharmaceutical, behavioral, boot camp regimens, nutritional, or simply "wars and lawsuits" to prevent use. Nancy Reagan is reported to have suggested: "Just say no." And the more the drug and alcoholism abuses proliferate, it seems that those—just like the original pioneers—who were required to say "no" (and did so), ask God's help, consort with likeminded believers, and help others, may have a better starting place than I ever had. I never said "no." But, when I was totally licked, I was quite willing to dive into A.A. as it was in 1986, see it as allowing for my own understanding of Almighty God, fervently ask God for help, and work toward the ideas of love and service that Dr. Bob proclaimed to be the essence of the program.

The post-Big Book publication changes—one and all—provide solid reasons for returning to, re-examining, and learning early ideas and history. As well as the changes that occurred after that program was developed and then described in 1938 by Frank Amos.

AA OF AKRON rides again through its four later pamphlets commissioned by Dr. Bob

I don't think anything surprised me more as an AA from the West Coast than finding the four AA OF AKRON pamphlets on sale at the Akron A.A. Intergroup Office--pamphlets said originally to have been commissioned by Dr. Bob as "Blue Collar A.A." pamphlets for the fellowship which, Dr. Bob had allegedly explained, were needed because "the Big Book was too complicated for many AAs" and Bob "wanted Evan [the designated writer] to present the program in its most basic terms." See Wally P. *But For The Grace Of God*, pp. 35-43.

These pamphlets, I was told at the Akron Intergroup Office, had apparently been around for years. They were filled with the kind of original Akron A.A. I've described above. They quoted the Bible, recommended prayer, discussed the importance of God, and did so in the context of the Twelve Steps. Yet how in the world did these gems come into being when their contents were virtually unknown where I came from out West? They seemed at first to be the product or property of some "clandestine A.A." until I learned what I know today—that they closely resembled the Frank Amos summary of early A.A. Old timer Mel B. told me recently that these were materials given to him when he entered A.A. in the late 1940's.

I can't say and do not know how much research has been done on their origins. But four have surfaced. Yet, for those who have become acquainted with early A.A. in Akron, there's not a surprise in them even though two of the four I own were republished, respectively in 1989 and 1993, while the other two were republished in October, 1997.

Treat yourself to this A.A. program material. Program principles and practices that were *not written by Bill W.,* that square with the A.A. that Frank Amos summarized, that frequently quote the Bible—just as Dr. Bob did, and that I described in detail above. And let's look at the general ideas in each of the pamphlets, one by one:

Spiritual Milestones in Alcoholics Anonymous

At the outset, this pamphlet asks and answers the following:

> But, asks the alcoholic, where can I find a simple, step-by-step religious guide? The Ten Commandments give us a set of Thou Shalts and Thou Shalt Nots; the Twelve Steps of AA give us a program of dynamic action; but what about a spiritual guide? Of course the answer is that by following the Ten Commandments and Twelve Steps to the letter we automatically lead a spiritual life, whether or not we recognize it.

Then the pamphlet says: "Here, however, is a set of suggestions, couched in the simplest of language:

> 1 – Eliminate sin from our lives.
> 2 – Develop humility

3 – Constantly pray to God for guidance.
4 – Practice charity.
5 – Meditate frequently on our newly found blessings, giving honest thanks for them.
6 – Take God into our confidence in all our acts.
7 – Seek the companionship of others who are seeking a spiritual life.

And the explanatory discussions of these seven points frequently mention God, Christianity, the Bible, and prayer. The pamphlet gives several illustrations of how men have found God. It concludes with the Prayer of St. Francis of Assisi.

A Manual for Alcoholics Anonymous.

This guide picks up the trail where *Spiritual Milestones* left off. It addresses the newcomer, hospitalization, sponsors, visiting the hospital, and what the newcomer must do on his discharge. He is told to read the Bible and give particular attention to the Sermon on the Mount, Book of James, 1 Corinthians 13, and the Twenty-third and Ninety-first Psalms. The guide suggests a prayer life for each and every day. Then it describes the thrill of helping someone else. Citing Matthew 6:34 of the Sermon on the Mount, it suggests day by day progress and acquiring health "one day at a time." [Anne Smith used this very quote and idea in her Spiritual Journal]. The pamphlet quotes Step Twelve as a "Spiritual Experience," not the "Awakening" Bill was soon to substitute as the result of taking the steps.

Second Reader for Alcoholics Anonymous

Its primary topic is, WHAT IS THERE IN AA FOR ME BESIDES SOBRIETY. And the article discusses four items: "Work, Play, Love, and Religion"—substituting A.A. for the latter. It contends that the good active AA is practicing Christianity whether he knows it or not. It devotes a paragraph to the Bible accounts that children loved for years: The Lord's Prayer, David and Goliath and Samson, Adam and Eve in the Garden, the Prodigal Son, and the Good Samaritan. [Clarence Snyder used to regale AAs and their families with his Bible stories about Noah, the Prodigal Son, and Adam and Eve. See Dick B., *That Amazing Grace: The Role of Clarence and Grace Snyder in*

Alcoholics Anonymous.] And the *Second Reader* lays out some very practical and purposeful ways of sharing a story in A.A. meetings.

A Guide to the Twelve Steps of Alcoholics Anonymous

With this fourth pamphlet, Akron AA completes the circle of A.A. activity. It offers the following as a simplified, condensed form of the complete program:

- We honestly admitted we were powerless over alcohol and sincerely wanted to do something about it. In other words, we admitted we were whipped and had a genuine desire to QUIT FOR GOOD.
- We asked and received help from a power greater than ourselves and another human. (NOTE: In almost all cases that power is called God. It is, however, God as WE UNDERSTAND HIM. . . .)
- We cleaned up our lives, paid our debts, righted wrongs.
- We carried our new way of life to others desperately in need of it.

The pamphlet discusses each of the Twelve Steps individually. It concludes with these rules for living.

- Remember that you are an alcoholic, and but one drink away from drunkenness again.
- Remember that you are completely dependent on God as you understand Him.
- Remember to keep your thinking straight.
- Remember that a wrong act will play on your mind until you either do something to rectify it or get drunk.
- Remember that defects will creep into your life if given half a chance.
- Remember that if only through gratitude, we must help others in order to help ourselves.

Conclusion

The Twelve Step member who studies, learns, and utilizes our history has a leg up on today's approaches to recovery. Many of these approaches ignore Jim Houck's sage observation as to A.A. that if you take God out of A.A. you have nothing.

For a Christian Twelve Step member: Knowing that A.A. began primarily with the ideas of Christian Endeavor and embraced conversion, Bible study, prayers, Quiet Hour, oodles of Christian literature, and the Biblical principles of love and service, he can find himself at home with any of these ideas he holds or wants to hold.

For those wanting to seek, find, and experience the original solution: Knowing that the original solution to alcoholism in Bill Wilson's mind was a conversion. And that the particular conversion involved a decision for Christ on one's knees usually after hearing that "Jesus saves;" voluntarily going to the altar to accept Jesus as Lord; participating in hymns, prayers, and Bible reading; and the penitent's leaving with the impression he had been made whole and was a forgiven child of the one, true, living Creator. This means that those who seek, receive, and espouse conversion can feel at home with their acknowledged Christian sonship.

For those catalyzed into historical witnessing: Knowing that the original Akron A.A. fellowship was considered a Christian Fellowship, emphasized Bible study, engaged in group prayers, discussed Biblical topics, heard from counselors like Anne Smith and Henrietta Seiberling, and insisted on a conversion followed by witnessing to those still suffering, those who wish to do likewise in A.A. can feel comfortable and reject intimidation for so doing.

For justified expectation of healing and cure: Knowing that the real origins of A.A. stemmed from: centuries-long accounts of divine healings; strong belief in the power, love, guidance, and forgiveness of God, understanding that coming to God meant accepting His son as Saviour, and recognizing that their effective witness was that God had done for the penitent what he could not do for himself, believers today can expect the same healing and cures attained by early AAs.

For appreciating the importance of historical material: Knowing that the Twelve Steps and Big Book were non-existent when A.A. was achieving great successes, the penitent can feel comfortable today in learning the Steps' Biblical origins, their shortcomings, and their utility as guides to moral, in fact Christian, behavior standards.

For understanding much-needed tolerance: Realizing that A.A. had never insisted on a particular church or sect or particular piece of literature, the person who seeks, talks about, understands, and discusses A.A. history can still feel tolerant whenever and wherever individual views, contrary to his own, are expressed by another. So long as done in the interest of sobriety—particularly if expressed in what Bill Wilson called our code of "love and tolerance."

For enthusiasm about Dr. Bob's Love and Service: Knowing our origins; refusing to entertain exclusionary rules as to people or beliefs; and recognizing that love of, and service to, our Creator, as well as love of, and service to, one's neighbor are keys to a harmonious joining in A.A.'s one-on-one program, long-time AAs can still proudly and effectively enable sick people to find God, to establish a relationship with Him, and to endeavor living according to His commandments and the principles taught in His Word and by His Son.

END

Gloria Deo

Bibliography

Alcoholics Anonymous, New Jersey: Works Publishing Company, 1939 [the "First Edition"]

Alcoholics Anonymous, 2d ed. NY: Alcoholics Anonymous World Services, Inc., 1956

Alcoholics Anonymous, 3rd ed. NY: Alcoholics Anonymous World Services, Inc., 1975

Alcoholics Anonymous, 4th ed. NY: Alcoholics Anonymous World Services, Inc., 2002.

Alcoholics Anonymous Comes of Age. NY: Alcoholics Anonymous World Services, Inc., 1957.

A Guide to the Twelve Steps of Alcoholics Anonymous. Akron: AA of Akron, n.d.

A Manual for Alcoholics Anonymous, rev. ed. AA of Akron, 1989

A Program for You: A Guide to the Big Book's Design for Living. Center City, MN: Hazelden, 1991.

AA Grapevine, The: "RHS" - issue dedicated to the memory of the Co-Founder of Alcoholics Anonymous, DR. BOB. NY: The AA Grapevine, Inc., 1951.

Allen, A. A. *How to Have Power Over the Devil*. AZ: A. A. Allen Revivals, Inc., 1954.

Almond, Harry J. *Foundations for Faith*. 2d ed. London: Grosvenor Books, 1980.

Allen, James. *As a Man Thinketh*. NY: Peter Pauper Press, Inc., n.d.

Anderson, Bernard W. *Understanding the Old Testament.* NJ: Prentice Hall, 1957.

A Newcomer Asks . . . York, England: A.A. Sterling Area Services, n.d.

As Bill Sees It: The A.A. Way of Life . . . selected writings of A.A.'s Co-Founder. NY: AAWS, 1967.

B., Dick. *Anne Smith's Journal, 1933-1939*, 3rd ed. Kihei, HI: Paradise Research Publications, Inc., 1998

_____. *By the Power of God: A Guide to Early A.A. Groups & Similar Groups Today*. Kihei, HI: Paradise Research Publications, Inc., 2000.

_____. *Cured!: Proven Help for Alcoholics and Addicts*. Kihei, HI: Paradise Research Publications, Inc., 2003.

_____. *Dr. Bob and His Library*, 3rd ed., Kihei, HI: Paradise Research Publications, Inc., 1998

_____. *God and Alcoholism: Our Growing Opportunity in the 21st Century*. Kihei, HI: Paradise Research Publications, Inc., 2002.

_____. *Good Morning!: Quiet Time, Morning Watch, Meditation, and Early A.A.*, 2d ed. Kihei, HI: Paradise Research Publications, Inc., 1998.

_____. *Henrietta Seiberling: Ohio's Lady with a Cause*. Kihei, HI: Paradise Research Publications, Inc., 2004.

_____. *Hope: The Story of Geraldine O. Delaney and Alina Lodge*, 2d ed. (Tincture of Time Press).

_____. *Making Known the Biblical History and Roots of Alcoholics Anonymous.* Kihei, HI: Paradise Research Publications, Inc., 2006.

_____. *New Light on Alcoholism: God, Sam Shoemaker, and A.A.*, 2d ed. Kihei, HI: Paradise Research Publications, Inc., 1999.

_____. *The Akron Genesis of Alcoholics Anonymous*, 2d ed. Kihei, HI: Paradise Research Publications, Inc., 1998.

_____. *The Books Early AAs Read for Spiritual Growth*, 7th ed. Kihei, HI: Paradise Research Publications, Inc., 1998.
_____. *The Conversion of Bill W.: More on the Creator's Role in Early A.A.* Kihei, HI: Paradise Research Publications, Inc., 2006.
_____. *The First Nationwide A.A. History Conference*. HI Paradise Research Publications, Inc., 2005
_____. *The Golden Text of A.A.: God, the Pioneers, and Real Spirituality*. Kihei, HI: Paradise Research Publications, Inc., 1999.
_____. *The Good Book and The Big Book: A.A.'s Roots in the Bible*, 2d ed. Kihei, HI: Paradise Research Publications, Inc., 1997.
_____. *The Good Book-Big Book Guidebook.* HI: Paradise Research Publications, Inc., 2006.
_____. *The James Club and The Original A.A. Program's Absolute Essentials* HI: Paradise Research Publications, Inc., 2006.
_____. *The Oxford Group and Alcoholics Anonymous*, 2d ed. Kihei, HI: Paradise Research Publications, Inc., 1998.
_____. *That Amazing Grace* (Clarence & Grace S.). Kihei, HI: Paradise Research Publications, Inc., 1996.
_____. *Turning Point: A History of Early A.A.'s Spiritual Roots and Successes.* Kihei, HI: Paradise Research Publications, Inc., 1997.
_____. *Twelve Steps for You.* HI: Paradise Research Publications, Inc., 2005)
_____. *Utilizing Early A.A.'s Spiritual Roots for Recovery Today*, Rev. ed. Kihei, HI: Paradise Research Publications, Inc., 1999.
_____. *When Early AAs Were Cured and Why*. HI: Paradise Research Publications, Inc., 2006.
_____. *Why Early A.A. Succeeded: The Good Book in Alcoholics Anonymous Yesterday and Today (A Bible Study Primer*). Kihei, HI: Paradise Research Publications, Inc., 2001.
B., Mel. *New Wine: The Spiritual Roots of the Twelve Step Miracle*. Hazelden, 1991
_____. *Ebby: The Man Who Sponsored Bill W.* Center City, MN: Hazelden, 1998.
_____. *My Search for Bill W.* Center City, MN: Hazelden, 2000.
Begbie, Harold. *Life Changers*. NY: G. P. Putnam's Sons, 1927.
_____. *The Gospel Truth: Life of William Booth, Founder and First General of the Salvation Army*, 2 vol. (New York: Macmillan, 1920)
_____. *Twice Born Men.* NY: Fleming H. Revell, 1909.
Benson, Clarence Irving. *The Eight Points of the Oxford Group*. London: Humphrey Milford. Oxford University Press, 1936.
Best of the Grapevine, Volume II. NY: The AA Grapevine, Inc., 1986.
Bobgan, Martin and Deidre. *12 Steps to Destruction: Codependency Recovery Heresies.* Santa Barbara, CA: EastGate Publishers, 1991.
Borchert, William G. *The Lois Wilson Story: When Love Is Not Enough*. Center City, Center City, MN: Hazelden, 2005.
Boardman, William. The Great Physician (Boston: Willard Tract Repository, 1881)
Bosworth, F. F. *Christ the Healer*. MI: Fleming H. Revell, 1996.
Brown, Kenneth O. *Holy Ground, Too: The Camp Meeting Family Tree.* PA: Holiness Archives, 1997.
Brown, William. *Personality and Religion*. London: University of London Press, 1946.
Bruns, Roger A. *Preacher Billy Sunday and Big-Time American Evangelism.* Urbana, IL: University of Illinois Press, 1992.
Buchman, Frank N. D. *Remaking the World.* London: Blandford Press, 1961.

Bufe, Charles. Alcoholics Anonymous: Cult or Cure? 2d ed (Tucson, AZ: See Sharp Press, 1998).
Burns, Dr. Cathy. *Alcoholics Anonymous Unmasked: Deception and Deliverance.* Mt. Carmel, PA: Sharing, 1991.
Bushnell, Horace. *The New Life.* London: Strahan & Co., 1868.
C., Stewart. *A Reference Guide to the Big Book of Alcoholics Anonymous*. Seattle: Recovery Press, 1986.
Cabot, Richard C., and Russell L. Dicks. *The Art of Ministering to the Sick.* NY: The Macmillan Company, 1946.
Carruthers, Donald W. *How to Find Reality in Your Morning Devotions*. Pennsylvania State College, n.d.
Chambers, Oswald. *My Utmost for His Highest.* Oswald Chambers Publishing Assn., 1963.
_____. *Studies in the Sermon on the Mount.* MI: Discovery House, 1960.
Cheever, Susan. *My Name is Bill W.* NY: Washington Square Press, 2004..
Clapp, Charles, Jr. *The Big Bender*. NY: Harper & Row, 1938.
Clark, Francis E. *Christian Endeavor in All Lands.* N.p.: The United Society of Christian Endeavor, 1906.
_____. *Memoirs of Many Men in Many Lands: An Autobiography*. Boston: United Society of Christian Endeavor, 1922.
Clark, Glenn. *How to Find Health through Prayer*. NY: Harper & Row, 1940.
Cleveland Central Bulletin. Volumes I - III Cleveland Central Committee, Oct/42 - Dec/45.
Clinebell, Howard. *Understanding and Counseling Persons with Alcohol, Drug, and Behavioral Addictions.* Rev. and enl. ed. Nashville: Abingdon Press, 1998.
Comparative Study Bible. Rev ed. MI: Zondervan Publishing House, 1999.
Complete Jewish Bible. Clarksville, MD: Jewish New Testament Publications, Inc., 1998.
Cuyler, John Potter, Jr. *Calvary Church in Action.* NY: Fleming H. Revell, 1934.
Day, Sherwood Sunderland. *The Principles of the Group.* Oxford: University Press, n.d.
Daily, Starr. *Recovery*. Minnesota: Macalester Park Publishing, 1948.
_____. *Release*. NY : Harper & Brothers, 1942
Darrah, Mary C. *Sister Ignatia: Angel of Alcoholics Anonymous*. Chicago: Loyola University Press, 1992.
Dawson, George Gordon. *Healing: Pagan and Christian.* London: Society for Promoting Christian Knowledge, 1935.
Day, Sherwood Sunderland. *The Principles of the Group.* Oxford: University Press, n.d.
Dearmer, Percy. *Body and Soul: An Enquiry into the Effects of Religion Upon Health, With a Description of Christian Works of Healing From the New Testament to the Present Day*. London: Sir Isaac Pitman & Sons, Ltd., 1909.
Dowling, Edward, S.J. *Catholic Asceticism and the Twelve Steps.* St. Louis MO: The Queen's Work, Brooklyn, 1953.
DR. BOB and the Good Oldtimers. NY: Alcoholics Anonymous World Services, Inc., 1980.
Drummond, Henry. *The Greatest Thing in the World.* Fleming H. Revell, 1968.
_____. *The Ideal Life*. NY: Dodd, Mead and Company, 1898.
Dubiel, Richard M. *The Road to Fellowship*. NY: iUniverse, Inc., 2004.
Dunn, Jerry. *God is for the Alcoholic*. Chicago: Moody Press, 1965.

E., Bob. *Handwritten Note to Lois Wilson on pamphlet entitled "Four Absolutes."* (Copy made available to author by Founders Day Archivist, Akron, Ohio, in June, 1991)
_____. *Letter from Bob E. to Nell Wing.* NY: Stepping Stones Archives, Bedford Hills, NY.
Eddy, Mary Baker. *Science and Health with Key to the Scriptures.* Boston: Published by the Trustees under the Will of Mary Baker Eddy, 1916.
Ellis, William T. *Billy Sunday: The Man and His Message.* Chicago: Moody Press, 1959.
Fillmore, Charles. *Christian Healing.* Kansas City: Unity School of Christianity, 1936.
Fillmore, Charles and Cora. *Teach Us to Pray.* MO: Unity School of Christianity, 1945.
Finch, Cora. Carl Jung, *A New England Family, and the Risks of Anecdote*, 2006.
Findlay, James F., Jr. *Dwight L. Moody: American Evangelist 1837-1899* (Chicago: The University of Chicago Press, 1969)
Fitzgerald, Robert. *The Soul of Sponsorship: The Friendship of Father Ed Dowling, S.J,. and Bill Wilson in Letters.* Center City, MN: Hazelden, 1999.
Forde, Eleanor Napier. *Guidance: What It Is and How to Get It.* Paper presented by Eleanor Napier Forde at Minnewaska, New York, September, 1927.
_____. *The Guidance of God.* London: The Oxford Group, 1927.
Fosdick, Harry Emerson. *The Man from Nazareth: As His Contemporaries Saw Him.* NY: Harper & Brothers, 1949.
_____. *The Meaning of Prayer.* NY: Association Press, 1915.
Fox, Emmet. *Find and Use Your Inner Power.* NY: Harper & Brothers, 1937.
_____. *Getting Results by Prayer* (pamphlet, 1933).
_____. *Power through Constructive Thinking.* NY: Harper & Brothers, 1932.
_____. *The Sermon on the Mount.* New York: Harper & Row, 1934.
Frame, Hugh F. *Wonderful, Counsellor: A Study in the Life of Jesus.* London: Hodder And Stoughton Limited, 1935.
Frost, Evelyn. *Christian Healing: A Consideration of the Place of Spiritual Healing in the Church of To-day in the Light of the Doctrine and Practice of the Ante-Nicene Church.* London: A.R. Mobray & Co. Limited, 1940.
Gilkey, Charles Whitney. *Jesus and Our Generation.* Chicago: The University of Chicago Press, 1925.
Glover, T. R. *The Jesus of History.* New York: Association Press, 1930.
Grant, W. V. *Just Before the Healing Service.* TX: Faith Clinic, n.d.
_____. *Live all Your Life.* TX: Faith Clinic, n.d.
_____. *Power from on High.* TX: Faith Clinic, n.d.
_____. *The Grace of God in My Life.* TX: Faith Clinic, 1952.
_____. *When Prayer Fails.* TX: Grant's Faith Clinic, n.d.
Gray, Steve. *Hope Heals.* MO: World Revival Press, 2003.
Grensted, Rev. L. W, *Psychology and God: A Study of the Implications of Recent Psychology for Religious Belief and Practice.* London: Longmans, Green and Co., 1931.
_____. *Psychology and God: A Study of The Implications of Recent Psychology For Religious Belief and Practice (London: Longmans, Green and Co, 1931).*
_____. *The Person of Christ.* London: Nisbet & Co., Ltd., 1933.
Guldseth, Mark. *Streams.* Alaska: Fritz Creek Studios, 1982.
Harrell, David Edwin, Jr. *Oral Roberts: An American Life.* San Francisco: Harper & Row, 1985.
Harris, Irving. *The Breeze of the Spirit.* NY: The Seabury Press, 1978.

Hartigan, Francis. *Bill W.: A Biography of Alcoholics Anonymous Co-Founder Bill Wilson.* NY: St. Martin's Press, 2000.
Hayes, Norvell. *The Healing Handbook*. Tulsa, OK: Harrison House, 1982.
Heard, Gerald. *A Preface to Prayer*. NY: Harper & Brothers, 1934.
Heiler, Friedrich. *Prayer: A Study in the History and Psychology of Religion.* Oxford: Oneworld Publications, 1932.
Herman, E. *Creative Prayer.* London: James Clarke & Co., 1921.
Hicks, Roger. *How to Read the Bible*. London: Moral Re-Armament, 1940.
Hickson, James Moore. *Heal The Sick*. London: Methuen & Co., 1924.
Holm, Nora Smith. *The Runner's Bible.* NY: Houghton Mifflin Company, 1913.
Hunter, T. Willard. *World Changing through Life Changing*. Masters Thesis. MA: Andover-Newton Theological School, 1977.
Inman, Philip. *Christ in the Modern Hospital*. London: Hodder & Stoughton Ltd., 1937.
Howard, Peter. *Frank Buchman's Secret.* Garden City, NY: Doubleday & Co., 1961.
James, William. *The Varieties of Religious Experience*. NY: First Vintage Press/The Library of America Edition, 1990.
Jones, E. Stanley. *Christ and Human Suffering*. New York: The Abingdon Press, 1930.
_____. *The Christ of the Mount*. NY: Abingdon Press, 1930.
Jung, Carl Gustav. *Modern Man in Search of a Soul*. NY: Harcourt, Brace & World, Inc., 1933.
_____. *Psychology & Religion.* New Haven: Yale University Press, 1938.
_____. *The Psychogenesis of Mental Disease.* NY: Bolingen Foundation, 1960.
K., Mitchell. *How it Worked: The Story of Clarence H. Snyder and the Early Days of Alcoholics Anonymous in Cleveland, Ohio*: NY: AA Big Book Study Group, 1997.
K., Richard. *Early A.A--Separating Fact from Fiction: How Revisionists Have Led Our History Astray*. Haverhill, MA: Golden Text Publishing Co., 2003.
_____. *New Freedom: Reclaiming Alcoholics Anonymous. MA*: Golden Text Publishing Co., 2005
Kagawa, Toyohiko. *Love: The Law of Life.* Philadelphia: The John C. Winston Company, 1929.
Kelsey, Morton T. *Psychology, Medicine & Christian Healing.* Rev. ed. San Francisco: Harper & Row, Publishers, 1966.
Kenyon, E. W. *Jesus the Healer.* Kenyon's Gospel Publishing Society, Inc., 2000.
_____. *The True Story*. FL: Creation House, 1997.
_____. *The Wonderful Name of Jesus.* Kenyon's Gospel Publishing Society, 1998.
King, J. D. *"Written Not With Ink But With the Spirit."* MO: World Revival Press, 2003
Kitchen, V. C. *I Was a Pagan*. NY: Harper & Brothers, 1934.
Knippel, Charles Taylor. *Samuel M. Shoemaker's Theological Influence on William G. Wilson's Twelve Step Spiritual Program of Recovery (Alcoholics Anonymous*). Doctoral Dissertation. St. Louis University, 1987.
Kurtz, Ernest. Not-God: A History of Alcoholics Anonymous, Exp ed. Center City, MN: Hazelden, 1991.
Lake, Dr. John G. Lake. *The Astounding Diary of Dr. John G. Lake.* TX: Christ for the Nations, 1987.
Laubach, Frank. *Prayer (Mightiest Force in the World*). NY: Fleming H. Revell, 1946.
Laymon, Charles M. *A Primer of Prayer.* Nashville: Tidings, 1949.
Lean, Garth. *Frank Buchman: A Life*. London: Constable, 1985.

Lewis, C. S. *Miracles: How God Intervenes in Nature and Human Affairs*. NY: Collier Books, 1960.
Liardon, Roberts. *God's Generals*. Tulsa, OK: Albury Publishing, 1996.
_____. *John G. Lake: The Complete Collection of His Life's Teachings*. Tulsa, OK: Albury Publishing, 1999.
Lindsay, Gordon. *John Alexander Dowie: Champion of the Faith*. TX: Christ for the Nations, Inc., 1987.
_____. *John G. Lake: Apostle to Africa*. TX: Christ for the Nations, 2000.
_____. *The John G. Lake Sermons*. TX: Christ for the Nations, 2002
_____. *The New John G. Lake Sermons*. TX: Christ for the Nations, 1994.
_____. *William Branham: A Man Sent from God*. IN: William Branham Evangelistic Association, n.d.
Lovett, C. S. *Jesus Wants You Well!* Baldwin Park, CA: Personal Christianity, 1973.
Lupton, Dilworth. *Religion Says You Can*. Boston: The Beacon Press, 1938.
Macmillan, Ebenezer. *Seeking and Finding*. NY: Harper & Brothers, 1933.
Maillard, John. *Healing in the Name of Jesus*. London: Hodder & Stoughton, 1936.
Markey, Morris. "Alcoholics and God," *Liberty Magazine*, 1939.
McCarthy, Katherine. "The Emmanuel Movement and Richard Peabody" (*Journal of Studies on Alcohol*), Vol. 45, No. 1, 1984.
McIntosh, Ron. *The Quest for Revival: Experiencing Great Revivals of the Past, Empowering You for God's Move Today*. Tulsa, OK: Harrison House, 1997.
McPeek, Rev. Francis, Lecture 26, "The Role of Religious Bodies in the Treatment of Inebriety in the United States," *Twenty-nine Lectures with Discussions As Given at the Yale Summer School of Alcohol Studies*. New Haven: Quarterly Journal of Studies on Alcohol, 1945, p. 417)
Micklem, E. R. *Miracles & The New Psychology: A Study in the Healing Miracles of the New Testament*. London: Oxford University Press, 1922.
Mitchel, Dale. *Silkworth: The Little Doctor Who Loved Drunks*. Center City, MN: Hazelden, 2002.
_____. *Silkworth: The Little Doctor Who Loved Drunks (MN: Hazelden, 2002).*
Moody, Dwight L. *Secret Power: Or, the Secret of Success in Christian Life and Work*. Chicago: F. H. Revell, 1881.
Mosely, Rufus. *Perfect Everything*. MN: Macalester Park Publishing, 1949.
Mott, John R. *The Evangelization of the World in This Generation*. New York: Student Volunteer Movement for Foreign Missions, 1900.
Murch, James DeForest. *Successful C.E. Prayer-Meetings*. OH: Standard Publishing Co., 1930.
New Bible Dictionary, Second Edition. England: Inter-Varsity Press, 1982.
New Jerusalem Bible. New York: Doubleday, 1985
Newton, James Draper. *Uncommon Friends*. NY: Harcourt Brace, 1987.
Osborn, T.L. *Believers in Action*. Tulsa, OK: T. L. Osborn, 2000.
_____. *Healing the Sick*. Tulsa, OK: Harrison House, 1992.
_____. *Join This Chariot*. Tulsa, OK: Osborn Foundation, n.d.
_____. *Miracles: Proof of God's Power*. Tulsa, OK: Harrison House, 1981.
_____, and Daisy Osborn. *When Jesus Visited Our House*. Tulsa, OK: Faith Digest, 1960.
P., Wally. *But for the Grace of God*. WV: The Bishop of Books, 1995.
Parker, William R., and Elaine St. Johns. *Prayer Can Change Your Life*. New ed. NY: Prentice Hall, 1957.
Pass It On. NY: *Alcoholics Anonymous World Services*, 1984.

Paton, Wally. *How to Listen to God: A Guide to Successful Living through the Practice of Two-way Prayer*. Tucson, AZ: Faith With Works Publishing Company, 2000.
Peabody, Richard R. *The Common Sense of Drinking*. Atlantic Monthly Press Book, 1939.
Peale, Norman Vincent. *The Positive Power of Jesus Christ*. NY: Foundation for Christian Living, 1980
_____. *The Power of Positive Thinking*. NY: Peale Center for Christian Living, 1978.
Peele, Stanton. *Diseasing of America*. Lexington, MA: Lexington Books, 1989.
_____, and Charles Bufe, *Resisting 12-Step Coercion: How to Fight Forced Participation in AA, NA, or 12-Step Treatment*. Tucson, AZ: See Sharp Press, 1998.
Phillips, Rachel M. *Billy Sunday: Evangelist on the Sawdust Trail*. Barbour Books, 2001.
Pittman, Bill. *AA The Way It Began*. Seattle: Glen Abbey Books, 1988.
Pittman, Bill, and Dick B. *Courage to Change: The Christian Roots of the Twelve-Step Movement*. Center City, MN: Hazelden, 1994.
Playfair, William L. *The Useful Lie*. Wheaton, IL: Crossway Books, 1991.
Poe, Stephen E. and Frances E. *A Concordance to Alcoholics Anonymous*. NV: Purple Salamander Press, 1990.
Pridie, J. R. *The Church's Ministry of Healing*. London: Society For Promoting Christian Knowledge, 1926.
Puller, F. W. *The Anointing of the Sick in Scripture and Tradition, with Some Considerations on the Numbering of the Sacraments*. London: Society for Promoting Christian Knowledge, 1904.
Raphael, Matthew J. *Bill W. and Mr. Wilson: The Legend and Life of A.A.'s Cofounder*. MA: University of Massachusetts Press, 2000.
Rawson, F. L. *The Nature of True Prayer*. England: The Society for Spreading the Knowledge of True Prayer, 1918.
Redwood, Hugh. *God in the Shadows*. London: Hodder & Stoughton, 1934.
Richardson, Alan. *The Miracle-Stories of the Gospels*. London: SCM Press Ltd, 1941.
Rice, Rev. Otis. Lecture 28, "Pastoral Counseling of Inebriates," *Twenty-nine Lectures with Discussions as given at the Yale Summer School of Alcohol Studies*. New Haven: Quarterly Journal of Studies on Alcohol, 1945.
Riss, Richard M. *A Survey of 20th-Century Revival Movements in North America*. MA: Hendrickson Publishers, 1988.
Roberts, Oral. *Expect A Miracle: My Life and Ministry*. Nashville: Thomas Nelson Publishers, 1995.
_____. *Oral Roberts' Life Story*. Tulsa, OK: Oral Roberts, 1952.
Robertson, Nan. *Getting Better: Inside Alcoholics Anonymous*. NY: William Morrow & Co., 1988.
Rose, Cecil. *When Man Listens*. NY: Oxford University Press, 1937.
Rose, Howard J. *The Quiet Time*. NY: Oxford Group at 61 Gramercy Park, North, 1937.
Rotherham's Emphasized Bible. MI: Kregel Publications, 1994.
Russell, A. J. *For Sinners Only*. London: Hodder & Stoughton, 1932.
S., Clarence. *Going through the Steps*, 2d ed. Altamonte Springs, FL: Stephen Foreman, 1985.
_____. *My Higher Power–The Lightbulb*. 2d ed., Altamonte Springs, FL: Stephen Foreman, 1985

Schaer, Hans. *Religion and The Cure of Souls in Jung's Psychology*. NY: Bolingen Foundation, 1950.
Schaff, Philip. *History of the Christian Church, Volume I*, 3rd Revision (Grand Rapids., MI: Wm B. Eerdman's Publishing Company, 1890.
Schambach, R. W. *Demon Possession Today and How to Be Free.* TX: Schambach Revivals, Inc., 1992.
_____. *God's Guarantee to Heal You*. Tx: Schambach Revivals, 1991.
_____. *The Price of God's Miracle-Working Power.* TX: Schambach Ministries, Inc., 1991.
Second Reader for Alcoholics Anonymous. Akron: AA of Akron, n.d.
Shafto, G. R. H. *The Wonders of the Kingdom: A Study of the Miracles of Jesus.* NY: George H. Doran Company, 1924.
Shoemaker, Helen Smith. *I Stand By The Door: The Life of Sam Shoemaker*. NY: Harper & Row Publishers, 1967.
Shoemaker, Samuel M., Jr. . . *And Thy Neighbor.* Waco, TX: Word Books, 1967.
_____. *By the Power of God*. NY: Harper & Brothers, 1954
_____. *Calvary Church Yesterday and Today.* NY: Fleming H. Revell, 1936.
_____. "Calvary Mission." Pamphlet. NY: Calvary Episcopal Church, n.d.
_____. *Children of the Second Birth.* NY: Fleming H. Revell, 1927.
_____. *Confident Faith.* NY: Fleming H. Revell, 1932.
_____. *Extraordinary Living for Ordinary Men.* MI: Zondervan Publishing House, 1965.
_____. *Freedom and Faith.* NY: Fleming H. Revell, 1949.
_____. *God's Control*. NY: Fleming H. Revell, 1939.
_____. *How to Become a Christian*. NY: Harper & Row, Publishers, 1953.
_____. "How to Find God." *The Calvary Evangel*, July, 1957.
_____. *National Awakening*. NY: Harper & Brothers, 1936.
_____. *Realizing Religion*. NY: Association Press, 1923.
_____. *One Boy's Influence.* NY: Association Press, 1925.
_____. *Religion That Works.* NY: Fleming H. Revell, 1928.
_____. *Sam Shoemaker at His Best.* NY: Faith At Work, Inc., 1964.
_____. *So I Stand by the Door and Other Verses.* Pittsburgh: Calvary Rectory, 1958.
_____. *The Church Can Save the World.* NY: Harper & Brothers, 1938
_____. *The Conversion of the Church*. NY: Fleming H. Revell, 1932.
_____. *The Experiment of Faith*. NY: Harper & Brothers, 1957.
_____. *The Gospel According to You.* NY: Fleming H. Revell, 1934.
_____. *Twice-Born Ministers.* NY: Fleming H. Revell, 1929.
_____. *With the Holy Spirit and with Fire.* NY: Harper & Brothers, 1960.
Smith, Bob and Sue Smith Windows. *Children of the Healer.* IL: Parkside Publishing, 1992.
Speer, Robert E. *Studies of the Man Christ Jesus.* NY: Fleming H. Revell, 1896.
_____. *The Principles of Jesus.* NY: Fleming H. Revell Company, 1902.
Spiritual Milestones in Alcoholics Anonymous. Akron: AA of Akron, n.d.
Stadsklev, Julius. *William Branham: A Prophet Visits South Africa.* MN: Julius Stadsklev, 1952.
Stafford, Tim. "The Hidden Gospel of the 12 Steps." *Christianity Today*, July 22, 1991.
Stalker, James. *The Life of Jesus Christ*. NY: Fleming H. Revell, 1891.
Streeter, B. H. *The God Who Speaks.* London: Macmillan & Co., Ltd., 1936.
Streeter, B. H. (Editor). *The Spirit: God and His Relation to Man Considered From The Standpoint of Philosophy, Psychology And Art.* London: Macmillan And Co., 1919.

Taylor, Vincent. *The Formation of the Gospel Tradition: Eight Lectures.* London: Macmillan & Co. Ltd., 1964.
Temple, William. *Christus Veritas: An Essay*. London: Macmillan & Co Ltd., 1954.
The Book of Yahweh, 7th ed.. Abilene, TX: The Houses of Yahweh, 1994.
The Co-founders of Alcoholics Anonymous: Biographical sketches Their last major talks, 1972, 1975.
The Complete Parallel Bible. Oxford: Oxford University Press, 1993.
The Contemporary Parallel New Testament (Eight Translations). NY: Oxford University Press, 1997.
The Dead Sea Scrolls Bible. HarperSanFrancisco, 1999.
The Four Absolutes. Cleveland: Cleveland Central Committee of A.A., n.d.
The Language of the Heart, Bill W.'s Grapevine Writings. NY: The AA Grapevine, Inc., 1988.
The Layman with a Notebook. *What Is The Oxford Group.* London: Oxford University Press, 1933.
The New Way of Life. A.A. Cleveland: The Cleveland District Office of Alcoholics Anonymous, n.d.
The Revised English Bible, New Testament.
The Schocken Bible: Volume I (The Five Books of Moses). NY: Schocken Books, 1995.
The Tidings. March 24, 1943.
The Upper Room (Methodist quarterly periodical which began publishing in April, 1935).
Thomsen, Robert. *Bill W.* NY: Harper & Row, 1975.
Thornton-Duesbury, Julian. *Sharing*. The Oxford Group, n.d.
Three Old-timer Clarence Snyder Sponsees and Wives. *Our A.A. Faith Legacy.* FL: Came to Believe Pub., 2005.
Tileston, Mary W. *Daily Strength for Daily Needs*. Boston: Roberts Brothers, 1893.
Tournier, Paul. *The Healing of Persons*. NY: Harper & Row, Publishers, 1965.
_____. *The Person Reborn.* NY: Harper & Row, Publishers, 1966.
Towns, Elmer. Porter, Douglas. *The Ten Greatest Revivals Ever: From Pentecost to the Present.* MI: Servant Publications, 2000.
Trimpey, Jack. *Rational Recovery: The New Cure for Substance Addiction.* NY: Pocket Books, 1996.
Trine, Ralph Waldo. *In Tune with the Infinite*. NY: Thomas H. Crowell, 1897.
Vaillant, George E. *The Natural History of Alcoholism Revisited.* MA: Harvard University Press, 1995.
Troward, Thomas. *The Edinburgh Lectures on Mental Science*. NY: Dodd, Mead & Co., 1909.
Vine's Expository Dictionary of Old and New Testament Words. NY: Fleming H. Revell, 1981.
Walker, Richmond. *For Drunks Only*. Hazelden. n.d.
Walter, Howard A. *Soul Surgery*. Oxford: The Oxford Group, 1928.
Webb. Terry. *The Tree pf Renewed Life: Spiritual Renewal of the Church through the Twelve-Step Program*, NY: Crossroad, 1992.
Weatherhead, Leslie D. *Discipleship.* London: Student Christian Movement Press, 1934,
_____. *How Can I Find God?* London: Hodder & Stoughton, 1933.
_____. *Psychology and Life.* New York: Abingdon Press, 1935.
_____. *Psychology, Religion, and Healing.* NY: Abingdon-Cokesbury Press, 1951.
Wells, Amos R. *Expert Endeavor: A Text-book of Christian Endeavor Methods and Principles*. Boston: United Society of Christian Endeavor, 1911.

What Others Think of A.A. Akron: Friday Forum Luncheon Club, circa 1941.
White, Tom. *Bill W.: A Different Kind of Hero-The Story of Alcoholics Anonymous.* Boyds Mills Press, 2003.
White, William L. *Slaying the Dragon: The History of Addiction Treatment and Recovery in America.* Bloomington, IL: Chestnut Health Systems/Lighthouse Institute, 1998
Wigglesworth, Smith. *Smith Wigglesworth on Healing*. PA: Whitaker House, 1999.
Willitts, Ethel R. *Healing in Jesus Name.* Crawfordsville, IN: Ethel R. Willitts, Publisher, 1931.
Wilson, Jim. *Healing through the Power of Christ.* London: James Clarke & Co., Ltd., 1946.
Wilson, Lois. *Lois Remembers*. NY: The Al-Anon Family Group Headquarters, 1979
_____. ("Lois Remembers: Searcy, Ebby, Bill & Early Days." Recorded in Dallas, Texas, June 29, 1973, Moore, OK: Sooner Cassette, Side One).
Wilson, Bill. *Bill Wilson's Original Story.* Bedford Hills, NY: Stepping Stones Archives, n.d., a manuscript whose individual lines are numbered 1 to 1180.
_____. *Bill W. My First Forty Years.* MN: Hazelden, 2000.
_____. "How the Big Book Was Put Together." NY: A.A. General Services Archives. Transcript of Bill Wilson Speech delivered in Fort Worth, Texas, 1954
_____. "Main Events: Alcoholics Anonymous Fact Sheet by Bill." November 1, 1954. Stepping Stones Archives, Bedford Hills, New York.
_____. "I Stand by the Door." *The AA Grapevine.* NY: The A.A. Grapevine, Inc., February, 1967.
_____. "W. G. Wilson Recollections," September 1, 1954 manuscript, personally inspected by Dick B. at Stepping Stones Archives, Bedford Hills, New York.
Wing, Nell. *Grateful to Have Been There: My 42 Years with Bill and Lois, and the Evolution of Alcoholics Anonymous.* IL: Parkside Publishing Corporation, 1992.
Winslow, Jack. *When I Awake*. London: Hodder & Stoughton, 1938.
Worcester, Elwood, Samuel McComb, and Isadore Coriot. *Religion and Medicine: The Moral Control of Nervous Disorders.* NY: Moffat, Yard & Company, 1908.
Wright, Henry B., *The Will of God and a Man's Lifework*. NY: The Young Men's Christian Assn. Press, 1909.

INDEX

P

Q

R

S

T

W

About the Author

Dick B. writes books on the spiritual roots of Alcoholics Anonymous. They show how the basic and highly successful biblical ideas used by early AAs can be valuable tools for success in today's A.A. His research can also help the religious and recovery communities work more effectively with alcoholics, addicts, and others involved in Twelve Step programs.

The author is an active, recovered member of A.A.; a retired attorney; and a Bible student. He has sponsored more than one hundred men in their recovery from alcoholism. Consistent with A.A.'s traditions of anonymity, he uses the pseudonym "Dick B."

He has had twenty-eight titles published including: *Dr. Bob and His Library*; *Anne Smith's Journal, 1933-1939*; *The Oxford Group & Alcoholics Anonymous*; *The Akron Genesis of Alcoholics Anonymous*; *The Books Early AAs Read for Spiritual Growth*; *New Light on Alcoholism: God, Sam Shoemaker, and A.A.*; *Courage to Change* (with Bill Pittman); *Cured: Proven Help for Alcoholics and Addicts; The Good Book and The Big Book: A.A.'s Roots in the Bible*; *That Amazing Grace: The Role of Clarence and Grace S. in Alcoholics Anonymous*; *Good Morning!: Quiet Time, Morning Watch, Meditation, and Early A.A.*; *Turning Point: A History of Early A.A.'s Spiritual Roots and Successes, Hope!: The Story of Geraldine D., Alina Lodge & Recovery; Utilizing Early A.A.'s Spiritual Roots for Recovery Today; The Golden Text of A.A.; By the Power of God; God and Alcoholism; Making Known the Biblical History of A.A.; Why Early A.A. Succeeded*; *Comments of Dick B. at The First Nationwide A.A. History Conference; Henrietta Seiberling: Ohio's Lady with a Cause;* and *The James Club*. The books have been the subject of newspaper articles and reviews in *Library Journal*, *Bookstore Journal*, *The Living Church*, *Faith at Work*, *Sober Times*, *Episcopal Life*, *Recovery News*, *Ohioana Quarterly*, *The PHOENIX*, and *The Saint Louis University Theology Digest*. They are listed in the biographies of major addiction center, religion, and religious history sites. He has published over 150 articles on his subject, most posted on the internet.

Dick is the father of two sons (Ken and Don) and has two granddaughters. As a young man, he did a stint as a newspaper reporter. He attended the University of California, Berkeley, where he received his A.A. degree with Honorable Mention, majored in economics, and was elected to Phi Beta Kappa in his Junior year. In the United States Army, he was an Information-Education Specialist. He received his A.B. and J.D. degrees from Stanford University, and was Case Editor of the Stanford Law Review. Dick became interested in Bible study in his childhood Sunday School and was much inspired by his mother's almost daily study of Scripture. He joined, and was president of, a Community Church affiliated with the United Church of Christ. By 1972, he was studying the origins of the Bible and began traveling abroad in pursuit of that subject. In 1979, he became much involved in a Biblical research, teaching, and fellowship ministry. In his community life, he was president of a merchants' council, Chamber of Commerce, church retirement center, and homeowners' association. He served on a public district board and has held offices in a service club.

In 1986, he was felled by alcoholism, gave up his law practice, and began recovery as a member of the Fellowship of Alcoholics Anonymous. In 1990, his interest in A.A.'s Biblical/Christian roots was sparked by his attendance at A.A.'s International Convention in Seattle. He has traveled widely; researched at archives, and at public and seminary libraries; interviewed scholars, historians, clergy, A.A. "old-timers" and survivors; and participated in programs and conferences on A.A.'s roots.

The author is the owner of Good Book Publishing Company and has several works in progress. Much of his research and writing is done in collaboration with his older son, Ken, an ordained minister, who holds B.A., B.Th., and M.A. degrees. Ken has been a lecturer in New Testament Greek at a Bible college and a lecturer in Fundamentals of Oral Communication at San Francisco State University. Ken is a computer specialist and director of marketing and research in Hawaii ethanol projects.

Dick is a member of the American Historical Association, Research Society on Alcoholism, Alcohol and Drugs History Society, Organization of American Historians, The Association for Medical Education and Research in Substance Abuse, Coalition of Prison Evangelists, Christian Association for Psychological Studies, and International Substance Abuse and Addictions Coalition. He is available for conferences, panels, seminars, and interviews.

Good Book Publishing Company Order Form

(Use this form to order Dick B.'s titles on early A.A.'s roots and successes)

Qty.	Titles by Dick B.	Price	
____	*A New Way In*	$19.95 ea.	$ ______
____	*A New Way Out*	$19.95 ea.	$ ______
____	*Anne Smith's Journal, 1933-1939*	$22.95 ea.	$ ______
____	*By the Power of God: A Guide to Early A.A. Groups and Forming Similar Groups Today*	$23.95 ea.	$ ______
____	*Cured! Proven Help for Alcoholics and Addicts*	$23.95 ea.	$ ______
____	*Dr. Bob and His Library*	$22.95 ea.	$ ______
____	*Dr. Bob of Alcoholics Anonymous*	$24.95 ea.	$ ______
____	*God and Alcoholism*	$21.95 ea.	$ ______
____	*Good Morning! Quiet Time, Morning Watch, Meditation, and Early A.A.*	$22.95 ea.	$ ______
____	*Henrietta B. Seiberling*	$20.95 ea.	$ ______
____	*Introduction to the Sources and Founding of A.A.*	$22.95 ea.	$ ______
____	*Making Known the Biblical History and Roots of Alcoholics Anonymous*	$24.95 ea.	$ ______
____	*New Light on Alcoholism: God, Sam Shoemaker, and A.A.*	$24.95 ea.	$ ______
____	*Real Twelve Step Fellowship History*	$23.95 ea.	$ ______
____	*That Amazing Grace: The Role of Clarence and Grace S. in Alcoholics Anonymous*	$22.95 ea.	$ ______
____	*The Akron Genesis of Alcoholics Anonymous*	$23.95 ea.	$ ______
____	*The Books Early AAs Read for Spiritual Growth*	$21.95 ea.	$ ______
____	*The Conversion of Bill W.*	$23.95 ea.	$ ______
____	*The First Nationwide A.A. History Conference*	$22.95 ea.	$ ______
____	*The Golden Text of A.A.*	$20.95 ea.	$ ______
____	*The Good Book and the Big Book: A.A.'s Roots in the Bible*	$23.95 ea.	$ ______
____	*The Good Book-Big Book Guidebook*	$22.95 ea.	$ ______
____	*The James Club and the Original A.A. Program's Absolute Essentials*	$23.95 ea.	$ ______
____	*The Oxford Group and Alcoholics Anonymous*	$23.95 ea.	$ ______
____	*Turning Point: A History of Early A.A.'s Spiritual Roots and Successes*	$29.95 ea.	$ ______
____	*Twelve Steps for You*	$21.95 ea.	$ ______
____	*Utilizing Early A.A.'s Spiritual Roots for Recovery Today*	$20.95 ea.	$ ______
____	*When Early AAs Were Cured and Why*	$23.95 ea.	$ ______
____	*Why Early A.A. Succeeded*	$23.95 ea.	$ ______

(Order Form continued on the next page)

Good Book Publishing Company Order Form

(continued from the previous page)

Order Subtotal: $ ______

Shipping and Handling (S&H) **: $ ______

(** For Shipping and Handling, please add 10% of the Order Subtotal for U.S. orders or 15% of the Order Subtotal for international orders. The minimum U.S. S&H is $5.60. The minimum S&H for Canada and Mexico is US$ 9.95. The minimum S&H for other countries is US$ 11.95.)

Order Total: $ ______

Credit card: VISA MasterCard American Express Discover (circle one)

Account number: ______________________________ Exp.: ______

Name: ______________________________ (as it is on your credit card, if using one)

(Company: ______________________________)

Address Line 1: ______________________________

Address Line 2: ______________________________

City: ______________________________ State/Prov.: ___________

Zip/Postal Code: _____________ Country: ______________________

Signature: ______________________ Telephone: ________________

Email: ______________________________

No returns accepted. Please mail this Order Form, along with your check or money order (if sending one), to: Dick B., c/o Good Book Publishing Company, PO Box 837, Kihei, HI 96753-0837. Please make your check or money order (if sending one) payable to "Dick B." in U.S. dollars drawn on a U.S. bank. If you have any questions, please phone: 1-808-874-4876 or send an email message to: dickb@dickb.com. Dick B.'s web site: www.DickB.com.

If you would like to purchase Dick B.'s entire 29-volume reference set on early A.A.'s roots and successes (and how those successes may be replicated today) at a substantial discount, please send Dick B. an email message or give him a call.

Paradise Research Publications, Inc.
PO Box 837
Kihei, HI 96753-0837
(808) 874-4876
Email: dickb@dickb.com
URL: http://www.dickb.com/index.shtml
http://www.dickb-blog.com

21736020R00046

Made in the USA
Charleston, SC
28 August 2013